CIRCLE DANCING

Celebrating the Sacred in Dance

June Watts

Green Magic

This edition is published by

Green Magic
Long Barn
Sutton Mallet
TA7 9AR
England

Typeset by Academic + Technical, Bristol
Printed and bound by Antony Rowe Ltd, Chippenham

Cover production by Kay Hayden
k.design@virgin.net

ISBN 0 9547 2308 2

GREEN MAGIC

'We came whittling out of nothingness
scattering stars like dust
The stars made a circle
and in the middle we dance'.

Rumi

My thanks to Esbjorn Aneer for unconditional support and endless hours of formating and other electronic necessities; to Caroline Sherwood for encouragment and wise counsel; and to David Roberts for putting me right when I dived into areas I knew too little about!

Contents

Introduction

'...for dancing to be a meditation, not just a social shuffle round the
dance floor, it has to be total: we have to give it all we've got, getting
lost in it, including our minds.'

Louis Proto

I had my first experience of ecstatic dance in Tin Mill School at the
tender age of six or seven. It was some sort of 'dance happening', at
least it didn't develop into a performance, and it **did** take up the entire
and, to diminutive me, vast hall. The incident is an isolated one, either
side is blank, but that moment of supreme oneness with the dance is
still crystal clear. Several classes were amalgamated – there must have
been a staff shortage or a wet sports lesson – and everyone was assigned
a role to dance. All the exciting parts with names (we were moving some
story – a Fairy Tale I believe) were allotted first and then there were the
rest of us, the 'extras' as they are called in the film world, shifting in
embarrassment from foot to foot, twiddling pigtails waiting for the
teacher to come up with something, anything!

'June Watts – lightning!'

I have no idea if there were other names called to be lightning, all I
know is that when the music and action began I was off! The god of lightning entered me and I leapt and zoomed and streaked across the room,
deftly zigzagging through the moving mass of bodies; the whole event
was a 'happening' about lightning, no doubt of that, and I **was** lightning!
I was transported, exhilarated, and no wonder! – seven years of repressed
creativity and expression had at last been given an outlet. The music
ended and I floated reluctantly back to earthbound reality, surprised
that I had not been singled out as a star and praised for my definitive lightning performance.

I had to wait for the odd musical in my theatre career before there was any applause for me as a dancer *'Oh what a lovely war'*, *'The Boy Friend'* and pantomimes in repertory theatres, *'Winter's Tale'* and *'All's Well that Ends Well'* for the Royal Shakespeare Company. These were wonderful but too few and far between, and then in 1982, post theatre career and heavily into parenthood, I found the perfect dance form that was all I had ever imagined dance to be and so much more; Sacred Dance as it was then called, exploded into my life, allowing me to express all parts of myself, and once again, and without the limit of school bells, I knew dance ecstasy!

The thread of the Dance I took hold of in 1982 led me out of a co-dependent marriage, and through years of many kinds of healing as I journeyed to find and live my true spirit and authentic self. That journey continues to this day and I am constantly awestruck at the depth and heights that are available through this dance medium. The power of the Dance to transform and heal is constantly increasing as is its facility to open and empower and fulfil the dancers. I am inexpressibly grateful for the gift of the Dance, and that my feet were led on to this path of initiation; grateful for Bernhard Wosien, the founder of Sacred/Circle Dance, and for all the teachers and circles along the way. The Dance continues to be my passion, my healing and my bliss, and passing it on is both a privilege and a great joy.

Dancing in circles is the oldest known dance form, and many cultures, religions and groups have their own 'Sacred Dance'. This particular genre is a unique mixture of traditional dances from Europe and modern choreo-graphies. Though Sacred Dance was the original name it is currently called both 'Sacred Dance', and 'Circle Dance'. Bernhard Wosien named it Heilige Tanze – holy or healing dance. It was re-named 'Circle Dance' when it moved down to England, but some people, I am one, prefer to combine the two and call it – 'Sacred/Circle Dance'. It is frequently written with a 'slash' as Sacred/Circle Dance, which implies an either/or. As the word 'sacred' means 'whole',[*] this fuller name of Sacred/Circle Dance without the 'slash', more roundly conveys its unique essence as both the dance of the whole person – body, mind and spirit – and the Dance of the Sacred Circle of all life.[†]

---

[*] 'Sacred' derives from the latin 'sacer' – holy. In Old English 'holy' and 'whole' are synonymous.

[†] For clarity, throughout the book when I use the name 'Circle Dance' it is as a general, umbrella term to refer to what dancing circles get up to! 'Sacred Dance' refers to what the Findhorn Foundation call Circle Dance and is its original name in English. 'Sacred/Circle Dance' is the later alternative name for Circle Dance, and the one I use to refer to what I personally teach, as not all circles would consider what they do to be 'sacred'.

It is not connected with, nor does it spring from or represent any religion or set of beliefs; it **does** express universal themes and aspirations, and is spiritual in the widest sense.

This book is the culmination of living and working with Sacred/ Circle Dance for more than 20 years. It is based on the experiences, insights and teachings I have had on this dancing path of initiation. My respect for, and commitment to it has grown over the years. I am still moved by its power to gently transform energy and move people into community and into a deeper awareness of themselves as not only physical but also spiritual beings. It is a joy and a privilege to help spread this beautiful dance medium.

I want to make it clear that I do not represent or speak for any body or group or indeed for anyone other than myself. There are various interpretations of Circle Dance and ways of passing it on; the view expressed here is as Touchstone says in 'As You Like It' – '*A simple thing but mine own*' so all the opinions, theories and perceptions you will read here are conclusions that I, just one among many teachers of Circle Dance, have come to from my own personal learning and experience over the years.

1

So what *is* Sacred/Circle Dance?

> *'There is random, unaware movement and there is centred consciousness movement – and it is the latter that brings us to the state of one-pointedness, body awareness and present-centredness that is the essence of meditation.'*
>
> Louis Proto

In 1976, Bernhard Wosien, an extraordinary German Ballet Master who had a passion for traditional European dance, arrived at the spiritual community of Findhorn in Scotland with a number of the dances he had collected on his travels through Europe. He intuitively knew which dances contained energies that would be needed in our present world, and would help heal the rift between humanity and the earth, the separation between us and our roots. The dances came from the countries on the edge of Europe – The Balkans, Greece, Russia, and Ireland – where people were still aware of their traditions and where the connection to the earth was still strong.

It is as if these old dances contain a code, which, it seems Bernhard realised, needs to be broken so that their power can be released and made available to help us through the massive changes on the earth of these times.

So the ancient dances of Europe fused at Findhorn with the new 'Aquarian' energy manifesting there, with its emphasis on the coming together in groups and the guidance of spirit, and so 'Sacred Dance', as it was then called, was born. From those early days, when Bernhard passed on the old dances together with some of his own choreographies, to the committed few at Findhorn, the Dance has spread worldwide. There are now very few towns in Britain that do not boast at least one regular Circle Dance group, and there are circles throughout Europe, the US, Canada, Australia, New Zealand, Africa and South America.

Sacred/Circle Dance in a gentle healing way brings body, mind and spirit together. It relieves stress, releases creative energy and helps the dancer feel both centred and connected. It is meditation in movement. Newcomers are often jokingly warned that it can become addictive! It's easy to become 'hooked' for several reasons: the feeling of moving rhythmically in a circle is relaxing and, at the same time, energising; it is a form of dance that doesn't require any previous dance experience, as the steps are simple, carefully taught at the time and easily learnt; the music is a stimulating mix of many styles – traditional, classical, reggae, pop, ethnic etc.; and there is a sense of belonging, of community, of 'coming home' in Sacred/Circle Dance, of being a part of an organic whole, which is deeply satisfying.

Over the centuries we have become fragmented, split into pieces, both as individuals and as a race. Our society has lost this sense of community, of each individual being a part of and playing a role in the collective. Exploring ourselves as individuals has been a necessary part of our evolution and it is time now to reconnect, to heal the fragmented bits of the psyche and restore the wholeness: in other words, to bring back the circle. Sacred/Circle Dance does not claim to be healing but it does help restore the wholeness. It is without doubt therapeutic – it does make you feel better in every way and it opens doors!

There was a woman drawn to the Dance whose daughter had died some time before and whose life had consequently lost meaning. It had so devastated her that she'd been more or less housebound ever since. In her fifth or sixth session of dancing she had a powerful experience – her daughter appeared strongly to her during the last dance. It was the first time such a 'door' had opened for her. They saw each other clearly and had deep communication. 'Glowing' is the best way to describe this woman as she recounted it all to me at the end. From that evening on her life made sense and she was able to pick up the pieces again.

The dances teach or rather they 'educate' in the literal sense of the word – to lead forth, i.e. lead out what is already deeply known within. The energy generated in the Dance can bring up emotions that may have been blocked and this helps restore self-esteem, trust and intimacy, if early experiences have damaged these. The secret is to keep on dancing until the emotions are released; after they are gone all that is left is the dance, the dance of the sacred self.

The circle is a symbol for unity, for community. The dancers come together seeking re-connection and a harmony with All That Is; they come seeking to re-awaken the unity their ancestors experienced, and to re-establish magic in their lives. This is rarely a conscious seeking;

however, mostly people do just feel somehow 'drawn' to come to dance.

They hold hands and the circle moves as a unit so there are no worries about being watched, making a fool of themselves, or getting it 'wrong'! It's not about getting steps 'right' anyway, but about enjoying the spirit of the dances and the sense of oneness and peace that comes from moving rhythmically in a supportive circle.

The purpose of the Dance is to join with something greater than ourselves (in the sense of a wider community but also something greater than the personality self – the whole Self). Coming into the circle we move from self and our individuality into an experience of a bigger whole, something we ourselves create and that we share equally.

Each dancer has a slightly different perspective on the circle and a slightly different view of the centre, and a unique understanding of the whole. It is like the blind men who feel different parts of the elephant! Each one feels and interprets something but none of them are able to have an awareness of the entire elephant.

The circle is the oldest dance form on the earth. There is no hierarchy in a circle; a circle allows everybody, whatever age or background, to feel accepted as an equal, and as the circle moves, the dancers begin to feel safe and relaxed, a state which enables them to discover the joy of dancing – often for the first time.

Under the general umbrella of Circle Dance there are many different emphases dependant on the particular interest and focus of the teacher. Some have returned to the traditional dances and find a total experience through them. In these circles there is no centre altar nor is silence held at the end of any particular dance or dance session – to quote traditional dance teacher, David Roberts, you would not for example, ask 'well-oiled Romanian villagers to hold hands and feel the energies after dancing say an Arcanul (a fast intricate Romanian dance!). I, on the other hand, have moved towards a more spiritual, symbolic, ritual, and energetic focus in the Dance and while I do teach many folkdances (though I am in no way qualified to expound on traditional dance) generally the majority of dances in my sessions are modern choreographies.

There was criticism in the early days of what was happening in Sacred/Circle Dance from some folk dancers, some of whom had no direct experience of it. In 1988 extracts from two articles that appeared in the newsletter of the Society for International Fok Dance plus extracts from several letters in response were published, anonymously, in the Spring edition of Grapevine (the magazine of the Sacred/Circle Dance network, cf chapter on Expansion). This one is from the article that started the fur flying: '*Today they have perfected and exported an adulterated mock up of horas, kolos and horos, with the trade mark "Circle Dancing". But stranger than that they have concocted for the inner clique, an extra special carry-on called Sacred Dance.... We have our hands full in the SIFD (Society for International Folk Dance) just to stay alive. We can do without pollution of our stream and tradition*'.

An ex-Sacred/Circle dancer wrote in similar vein in the same newsletter:

> '*This unlikely mish–mash of Balkan dances and hocus-pocus ... steps of the original are commonly altered or simplified; national or regional style is as a rule never taught, and indeed is often frowned upon*' ...

The ball was quickly lobbed back but without the vitriol! One circle dancer's response was – '*Sacred Dance is alive and kicking; IFDS/SIFD is a museum, perhaps we're more like a nature reserve. Sacred/Circle Dance is too large, well established and important in its work to fear pressure from articles like these*'.

The ex-Sacred/Circle dancer quoted above, however, did go on to make a plea for tolerance – '*I believe that straightforward, unadorned folk dance is "sacred" because of its beauty, the innocent happiness we get from it, and its marvellous potential for bringing different races and nations together in peaceful activity*', and ended – '*Let the Circle Dancers and the SIFD members together build bridges, not walls*'.

So what is the difference between folkdance and Circle Dance? The crucial ingredient is the consciousness brought to Sacred/Circle Dance. I would say it's a question of **awareness**: awareness of the dynamic of the still centre – the Source – and the moving circle; awareness of the meaning of the steps and the dimensions beyond them; awareness of the energy generated. Predominantly it is the awareness of energy that makes Sacred/Circle Dance different.

We are in a sense learning and returning to an awareness and an understanding that was implicit to the people in the countries where these traditional dances originate. David Roberts says '*Dance next to a Greek or Romanian villager a few times and you have touched the fountain from which steps and style (and their choreography to their music) come...*'. Traditional dances grew organically out of the culture, the land, the life experience of the people, (the same may be said of the circle dances being choreographed today). In Circle Dance we are reclaiming this ancient awareness and wisdom which I refer to in the chapter on The History of the Dance as a 'tribal consciousess', 'a dreamilke state of oneness with all that is'; but what is I believe unique now, as a sequel to our journey of individuation, is the consciousness of what we are doing when we dance, the awareness of the energies generated and how to use them to assist global awakening.

Energy is what we are; indeed it is **all** we are. Modern physics has shown us what we have long felt, that every subatomic particle dances, in fact, **is** an energy dance, an endless energy dance of creation and destruction.

Two people focusing energy together double (at least) the power – raising it from the equivalent of five amps to ten or more amps. Take a group of focused people and the level bumps up, put them in a circle and then move the circle with focused intent, and you're off the scale!

An amoeba functions in an extremely limited way and expresses a very minimal consciousness; our personality could not manifest through one cell or just a few cells, it needs an enormous number of cells all working together in harmony to bring our consciousness into form. In the same way, certain energies or level of energies can come through just one person, but there are energies that need groups of people harmoniously together for expression. A circle moving consciously in dance raises the voltage to mega levels and powerful energies are generated to facilitate our evolution and the earth's transition.

The magic and the mystery of this sort of dancing is that there are other dimensions to it than there are in a purely physical type of dancing, as for example, Salsa. Any type of dance affects the emotional body too – moving to music does make you **feel** good, but in Sacred/Circle Dance there is much more! It clears the mind of chatter junk, it activates healthy emotions, it balances the physical body and brings the spirit into it, brings soul and body together; in other words it combs through the tangles and makes room for the dancer's radiant spirit to be in the body.

By 'mystery'* I mean there is more here than my logical mind can grasp, so while there may be clear historical symbolism in a dance, as with a grain planting dance, or a warriors' dance, or while there may be life symbolism in a dance, such as *'Here in these steps we are flowing smoothly with life, here in this section we encounter a drawback and then we pause to review ...'* or whatever the meaning in the steps may be, there is in Sacred/Circle Dance this other 'beyond words' dimension, where Great Mystery enters. The Dance has the potential to take us beyond what we think we are, if so we are willing.

---

* From mysterion (old Greek) – a sacred rite usually for initiates.

5

2

Bernhard Wosien
– the instigator of the Dance and my experiences of him

> *'What I have realised after a lifetime with dance is that dance is meditation in movement, a walking into silence where every movement becomes prayer.'*
>
> Bernhard Wosien

Bernhard Wosien was born under a Virgo sun in 1906 in an area of Germany that is now part of Poland. He was a classical dancer, a ballet master and choreographer. A teacher, too, a graphic artist and a painter, his passion was expressing the spirit in dance and drawing. He was one of the first to research the origins and meanings of the traditional dances of Europe. In 1960 he left the theatre to concentrate on teaching dance, and to travel so as to learn the old Greek and Yugoslavian dances in their countries of origin. He used traditional and circle dances as a way to foster group awareness, and his aim was to bring sacred dance back into the community, to help ordinary people in their everyday lives.

In 1976 he arrived at Findhorn at the invitation of Eileen and Peter Caddy, two of the three founder members of the community, who had felt for a long time that what Findhorn was lacking was dance and music. And Bernhard felt that Findhorn was *'soil ready prepared for what I want to sow'*. It was an auspicious meeting and developed into a fruitful relationship.

To the Findhorn group of dancers he taught both traditional dances, his own choreographies – ranging in style and mood from the lively childlike **King of the Fairies** to the deep order and focus of the **Sun Meditation** – and also, with them, presented dance performances such

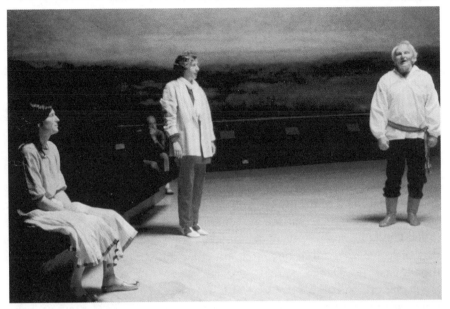

*Bernhard Wosien, Maria-Gabriele Wosien, and Ingrid Mann at the Findhorn
International Dance Festival 1986.*

as the Hymn of Jesus, and Theseus and the Minotaur, which were
compilations of both Folk dances and his choreographies.

A story I love to tell (it may be apocryphal but was told to me as
fact) is of Bernhard teaching **King of the Fairies** to the Findhorn
group. He told them a wondrous tale of the elements and a lake before
dawn and swans rising into the sunrise. After he left there was much
discussion and disagreement about what in fact he had said – people
remembered it differently, so when he returned for his next annual
visit there was a clamour of requests for the **King of the Fairies** story:
he told them a completely different tale!

Short on memory, or a Master? To me this is the Master, the
Teacher, saying it doesn't matter whether it's swans or magpies, don't
get hung-up on the image and miss the message, the map is not the
terrain, listen to what is truly true.

In the Spring 2002 edition of Grapevine, Keith Armstrong, writing
of his first meeting with Bernhard at Findhorn, tells how he saw Bernhard enter the room where they were to dance – '*The whole of his
centre of gravity moved from slumped somewhere near his belly to the centre of
his chest. Suddenly Bernhard was light and nimble on his feet, and transformed
from an aged figure into the spirit of youth in dance*'. Keith goes on to talk of

what he learned during that week in Findhorn, how Bernhard '*emphasised on all occasions the importance of dance*' as a means of devotion, and that the purpose of the dance was to join with something greater than ourselves. '*When we enter the circle we subsume the self and our individuality into the greater whole. We become part of something greater, something we each share, and share in equal measure. Each of us holds our place in the circle facing the centre. Each of us is attached to the centre, and shares the centre in common with everyone else. But each has a unique perspective and no link is the same as any other*'.

In summer 1986 to our great surprise and delight, Colin Harrison (who was spreading the Dance like wildfire south of the Scottish border) and I were invited to the International Dance Festival as guests of Findhorn. We were to be representatives, it seemed, of this slightly dubious offspring called Circle Dance. We were delighted by this softening of attitude feeling that once we were all in one circle together differences would dissolve in the unity of the Dance.

The great thrill for me was, at last, to have an opportunity to dance with Bernhard. (The last chance, as it turned out, as he died a few months later.) To be informed just before the festival, that though he would be present he would not be able to dance, as he had suffered another stroke, was devastating! But there was no stopping him: whatever the doctors may say, as long as there was breath in his body that man would dance. He **was** dance! It was even more riveting because he was physically limited. Awe-inspiring to watch this powerful stocky figure, still so muscular and physical, dancing minimally, etching in a line, suggesting a spiral, and with barely discernible movement creating – out of nothing as it seemed – a dance of the universe, of life, death, transcendence, a dance I could see and feel!

Three very personal memories of Bernhard have stayed with me from that week. The first was during a high-energy evening of dancing to live music in Cluny ballroom. The hall was crowded and buzzing. Bernhard's dance **King of the Fairies** was announced and Anna Barton asked me to lead the 'air' the third time through.

This is a dance of the elements and when it comes to the air section, the 'leader' opens the circle and leads the line around the room diving under the arms of the last two dancers and aiming to get the whole thing back in circular formation for the element of fire and the rising of the sun.

I was ecstatic! What an honour to be trusted to lead Bernhard Wosien and the entire circle on this journey. Surely this was the high point, if not the *raison d'être*, of my whole life! Off I went, in my element, swooping and swirling, an inspired breeze if ever there was one!

Bernhard Wosien teaching at the Findhorn International Dance Festival 1986.

Suddenly I sense a commotion! Looking back I see Bernhard, also 'swooping and swirling' at the head of his own 'breakaway' line of giggling dancers. 'NO!' I want to stop the dance and shout 'Anna, tell Bernhard that he's got it wrong, it's my turn, he was no.1 wind, **I'm** no.3 wind!' Of course there was no way I could do that and Bernhard continued to dance on blissfully unaware of the approaching crisis of the imminent sunrise.

Those first few moments were some of the worst, not the best, moments of my life simply because I was resisting what was happening. As soon as I relaxed and accepted the situation and realised that all I could do was keep on dancing it was fine, and somehow, through all the laughter and the chaos, two circles did manage to make it to the sunrise – almost on time. Or rather two circles celebrated **two** sunrises side by side and the hall was filled with cheers and laughter!

There was no knowing how aware Bernhard was of the situation – he appeared not to be – but it was an important gift for me, a lesson in surrendering expectations, ego and 'shoulds' to the Dance, trusting the process and going with the moment!

The second memory is from much later the same evening. I am in the bus on the way back from Cluny to the Park, two areas of the Findhorn Community roughly five miles apart (I'm using the present tense as

9

it is still present for me). Bernhard with his daughter, Maria-Gabriele, is in the seat in front of me and I'm sitting alone. Without turning round, he slips his arm between the seats and takes one of my hands in his and holds it firmly for those five timeless miles. I didn't move a muscle and hardly breathed the whole time in case the magic was broken. Something happened to me on that journey! It was as if something was being transmitted through his hand, something that felt like an empowerment, like I was being given a very precious gift.

The image of the third memory is etched indelibly on my mind, my heart, my body, my being. It is of Bernhard leaving the Universal Hall to catch his plane at the end of the festival. He turns on the top step and with arms upraised bids us what did turn out to really be his final farewell. He is wearing a white shirt and he is smiling, and thankfully someone took a photo, which I treasure and which is still inspirational to me. In that moment he was for me the Angel, the Messenger of the Dance: in that gesture he was ascending, and bestowing on us the blessing of the Cosmic Dancer, he was empowering us, and at the same time leaving his spirit with us.

Quite a lot for one photo frame! That's how it was for me and has continued to be ever since. I shall always be grateful to have had the opportunity to have danced with and felt touched by such a Master. So many times since when we dance, I feel him as a guiding inspirational presence, and frequently at the end of an especially vibrant powerful evening, I have 'seen' him, huge and shining up there filling the centre of the circle.

3

First Steps

– my introduction to the Dance

'*The art of dancing is a symbol for the law that everything passes.*'

Bernhard Wosien

That my mother – a strict Methodist, daughter of a preacher, married to a preacher – suggested we went to that Mind Body Spirit Festival together sometime at the end of the 1960s was remarkable; that she was as enthusiastic about the whole event as I was, was amazing; that she felt the same passionate urge as I did to get on stage and join in that moving circle was miraculous. Later when the dancing path led me into places she could not reconcile with her beliefs it was a different story, but this first contact with Sacred Dance stays with me as a true response of her being; for that one day she seemed to me to move out of mind control and belief systems and follow her soul. I'm glad of that, whatever dark coils of the labyrinth followed.

My inner self leapt at the vision of that dancing circle up there on that Festival stage in Bristol all those years ago. I learnt the steps with those dancers; I felt them in my body. I knew I could do them, knew somehow I **was** doing them, and I wanted so much to have the courage to jump up and join in, but fear had too firm a hold then. I wanted this dancing to go on all day, forever. It made sense of everything! Life, somehow, fell into place. Something so deep and lonely inside me that ached and cried, now recognised a 'home', and 'kin'. If this magical thing could happen here then maybe there was a place on earth for me after all.

That seed went in deep and lay dormant for ten years while I re-invented myself – as a mother. How long and dark, and diverting, the coils of the labyrinth journey can be! Then one glorious May weekend, I re-united with the Dance and with myself! I had three children by

11

that stage, and as the eldest, at a local village school, was showing signs of an influence I did not value, I looked around for an alternative and settled on Rudolph Steiner's Waldorf Education, which seemed to offer a more holistic and earth-based approach to the business of children. I say 'seemed' as it turned out to be not all it had seemed and far from what I had been hoping for, but that's another story. Suffice to say that finding another educational system for the children meant moving house – from Stratford-upon-Avon and 'theatre land', to Gloucestershire and 'alternatives'!

It was at Hawkwood College on the outskirts of Stroud, Gloucestershire that I took hold of the thread I had only witnessed at that festival ten years before. The weekend was a celebration of dance of many kinds; I remember a Sufi style dancing – turning and turning like pictures I'd seen of the Whirling Dervishes – which took me high; I remember the joy of dancing a magnificent rainbow ribboned maypole as it was the time of Beltane, the May Day festival, but whatever other forms there may have been all were eclipsed by two hours of something called Sacred Dance! Bells went off! This was it, what I had been waiting for forever! I followed the teacher around all weekend pestering for more – How did that one go again? Can we have another session? Where can I do this again/for ever...?

The teacher was King of the Dancing Elves, a magical man on his way from my Dream Paradise no.1 (i.e. the herb garden at Findhorn) to take up guardianship of my Dream Paradise no.2, namely Chalice Well Gardens, Glastonbury. With those credentials of course I was going to be enthusiastic about anything he taught but – this was beyond the beyond of imagining!

Taras Kosikowsky – I have carried this name in my brain and the owner of it in my heart ever since! Meeting this man was a major turning point in my life – one of those moments when the clouds part and destiny dances before you.

He must have been airlifted in from the Land of Faerie. When he began to dance, I knew I was circling with one of Pan's people. Of **course** he was focalising the herb garden in the magic faraway world of Findhorn. What else would he be doing?

Taras handed me the thread of the Dance – Sacred Dance, as it was then known – and set my feet on a magical path in 1981. I followed it to Findhorn and halfway round the world, and into a new life. It has guided me through impossible thickets and continues to lead me through the labyrinth of my life. It keeps me on track. It is Ariadne's thread that leads me on the path into myself to recognise and to bring into the light the dark demons of my fears; it is the line of golden light from my soul that leads me home.

I'm still following it over twenty years on and it came full circle recently in the Growing Needs Bookshop in Glastonbury. There behind the counter was my way-shower, not dancing now but feeding growing needs in a different way. At last I was able to share with him the fruits of what he had unwittingly sown and to thank him.

No reason why he would have remembered me though – a millennium later – though he says he does! If so, what would he remember? A starry-eyed leech bombarding him with questions: *'Can you show me that Greek one again?' 'When can we have another session please?' 'Where can I learn more?'*

Taras spoke in Glastonbury of those far-off days with Bernhard in the 1970s when the Dance was seeded at Findhorn, and I thought, as I listened breathlessly – here I am in the presence of living Dance history. It was in Taras' caravan at the Park that the tapes Bernhard Wosien had brought with him were recorded. It was Taras' hand that had held the microphone! I felt excitement and awe at linking back with what had begun in that caravan, at the passion and dedication of those first few. I felt tenderness for the hand that had held that mike, and for the sounds of birdsong and car engines in the background of those first recordings. This was the first stirring of the seed that is still expanding into an ever more magnificent flower.

4

Findhorn – but no wellies!
(I get to Findhorn!)

> 'We know that when the Great Spirit created the world he did so by
> singing and dancing. The heartbeat of our Mother Earth was the drum
> that accompanied Him. We feel Her heartbeat when we lie down on
> the ground, when the Yumari planting dance is played.'
>
> Life in the eyes of a Tamahurara
> (Indian tribe of Northern Mexico)
> interpreted by Romayne Wheeler

So Findhorn was the Mecca of Sacred Dance! It had, ever since I first
heard of the place, certainly been a Mecca for me. One day I knew I
would pilgrimage there. At Findhorn a way of life I had always
dreamed of was actually happening; there the fairy world was being
recognised and worked with. I had read 'The Findhorn Garden' and felt
a thrill of recognition. It had opened up a whole sub stratum of my life
that was somehow managing to sustain me through nappies and shopping
and the mum humdrum. Fairies had been my friends as a child – until
shamed into putting away such childishness and told to 'Grow up!' I
had submerged the knowing of that world deep inside but suddenly,
miraculously I read a book written by **adults** who talked of fairies as
comfortably and confidently as Rose Elliott talked of cooking lentils.

So my dream, which I knew one day would become a reality, long
before I met Sacred Dance, was to go to Findhorn. I had a sense that I
would meet myself there though I never articulated it so clearly then –
there was just a strong feeling and an intense excitement in my guts
every time I heard the name. But the reality of my life was that I was
married to an actor, which meant I was a very part time wife and
virtually a single parent looking after three small children. You don't
expect to see your partner much if he's wedded to the theatre; actors

14

have to go where the work is and the hours don't leave much time for anything else, like relationships! This actor was contracted with the Royal Shakespeare Company, which had houses in Stratford-upon-Avon and London, but unfortunately not in Stroud, Gloucestershire. So dream on! Dreams were for exhausted night times when the kids were asleep.

But, then, once upon a time, in late spring, an angel popped into my kitchen, waved her magic wand (well maybe she was a Fairy Godmother!) and said *'You **shall** go to Findhorn!'*

She was a 'Steiner' mother, as I was – we had children in the same classes at the Waldorf School near Gloucester. She listened patiently to what was arranged for the children to do over the summer, then asked – *'and what about **you**, what are **you** doing?'* Baffled reaction! Me? Well, my job is making sure everyone else has a great summer. *'And what would you do if you could?'* *'Go to Findhorn of **course**, but of course I can't just **go**, and anyway we don't have the money'.* My 'fairy godmother' had just received a refund from the Electricity Board, which was, she said, surplus to requirements, i.e. the family didn't really **need** it! That day I began believing in miracles. The money she gifted me paid for the journey and part of the cost of Experience Week, a week geared to first timers to give them a taste of the life there and introduce the ethos of the community. It was also, and more importantly, an excursion into what lies beneath the personality mask, but I didn't know that then, all I knew was there would be huge cabbages and fairy folk.

Up in the rarefied Scottish air, the decision makers of the Findhorn community 'attuned' to my need and my commitment to get there somehow and granted me a bursary to complete the fees! My fate was sealed! Or to put that in a more positive way – my life would never be the same again!

It all fell into place, as things do when you're on track in your life, and so one summer morning in 1982, I set off, backpack on my back, with a dream to live. The universe always demonstrates support when you take a step clearly and strongly in answer to the soul's prompting. That morning I had confirmation – if one were needed – that I was on my life's track and that the universe was supporting me.

As I walked out of Gloucester Cathedral, where I had gone to prepare myself inwardly and spiritually for my pilgrimage, there came a noise like a *'rushing mighty wind'* and the sky darkened as the biggest congregation of birds I have ever seen flew over me, and not just me, over the cathedral and its entire sacred precincts. They completely filled the sky turning it black; the noise of the wings and the cheeping of those countless messengers was almost deafening. I felt myself soar with them and sent up a prayer of thanks for what I took to be a breath-taking send-off and blessing from the world of spirit. The auguries were good! My spirit was bursting with the joy of being on this adventure, following my star.

I **could** say that the highlight of my Findhorn Experience Week was a session of Sacred Dance and leave it at that. But the week was so much more than I had anticipated, and I can't, unlike Pooh, take the honey and leave the bread – the bread being intense inner work; the honey, the dancing. I cannot separate the two. When I dance, it's Me dancing! So the week gave me Dance and it gave me growing pains; it started a long, painful, dismantling of who I thought I was, while the Dance gave me glimpses of who I really am!

I didn't go to Experience Week expecting to dance – what I did expect was to be in close communion instantly with the nature spirits. I pictured myself lying blissed out in my wellies among the giant cabbages in the vegetable garden receiving messages from the devas. Of course this was why Findhorn had given me the bursary: they had 'seen' this when they tuned in! Naturally when the 'focaliser' (an American borrowing that has more or less replaced the word 'leader' which, I guess, is considered to be in conflict with the new group-community-equality ethic) handed out our morning work assignments for the week I assumed it would be the Garden.

But there were to be no wellies or cabbages or information from the devas for me. I got House Care and was detailed to cleaning the bar and loos for the week! *'No, there has to be a mistake! They've muddled me up with someone else!'* But 'they' are guided by spirit and don't make mistakes! Blazing with righteous indignation – *'I spend half my life doing house cleaning! Is **this** the dream? Have I come all this way and spent all my fairy godmother's electricity refund to do what I do every day at home?'* To cap it all I get the angel of Joy for the week! Ha! The right angel, yes, for wellie communing, certainly for the one blissful afternoon of Sacred Dance, but – House Care?

I realised later that, yes, I may have come to Findhorn to dance, but I had also come to begin an intensive quest for my true being, and these two strands are, for me, inseparable.

As dancers, we bring only ourselves. Musicians have their instruments, opera singers their vocal instrument, artists their brushes and paints, crafts people their tools; all of these require skill, years sometimes of learning and practice; a dancer simply has the body, **that** is the instrument. Ballet dancing demands an intensive training, it has a language that must be scrupulously learnt and the dancer must work daily on maintaining the necessary flexibility and technique. What then of Sacred/Circle Dance? We just show up, hold hands and off we go. Of course one of the great joys of this form of dance is that it **is** so accessible, that anyone may come in and be part of the circle; we are proud to advertise it as dancing that needs no training or previous experience of dancing.

However, there is another aspect to this and this is one place where I say the 'Sacred' comes in. Sacred/Circle Dance is not just a physical exercise; it works on the whole person, on all levels of the being – clearing the emotions, calming the mind, strengthening the presence of the spirit in the body. As a way of initiation it moves us towards full consciousness of ourselves and that means, if we embrace it fully, that we are constantly working on ourselves to release the out of date myths about who we are, dissolve the pain body and learn empowerment by judiciously **using** the mind rather than being a victim of it. In other words, if we follow it as our spiritual discipline, we cannot separate who we are from the Dance.

The first task of this conscious quest for myself was to learn to reconcile my angel with my assignment, and find joy in cleaning the toilets. And I did! I did turn it around and found great joy and satisfaction in performing that essential morning chore. It became a service – a gift – to the community. I took great pride in it and loved doing it – it truly

Dancing at the Pink House Findhorn. Bernhard Wosien in the middle in white shirt.

17

became an act of love. I was on the path of initiation to be a true holder of the thread of the Dance.

This is what I mean when I say we bring only ourselves and in this sense the word 'only' is misleading – it minimises the truth. We bring – into the temple – not a violin and the skill to play it, or oil paint and canvas, or amazing vocal techniques, we bring everything we are; we bring our entire vast being, nothing less will do as an offering to the Source of All.

5

Brief History of Dance
– to put Sacred/Circle Dance in context

'People, learn to dance, otherwise the angels in heaven will not know what to do with you.'

St Augustine

Unlike most other species on the planet we have always danced – fact one! Fact two – the most natural form in life is the circle. Everything natural moves in a cycle, travelling from a beginning, through a middle, to an ending which is another beginning, and yet a circle is seamless having neither beginning nor ending.

Above us is the wheel of the heavens, the great cosmic circle dance of sun and moon and stars. Around us is the cycle of the seasons – the springtime shoots, through the summer expansion and autumn harvest, to the dying down, the returning to the earth, the composting of the old out of which the new life emerges.

The ancient people knew time was a circle not a straight line, and that there were special points on the circle that called for ritual and celebration. These are 'stations' in the cycles of the Sun, the Earth and the Moon – the journey of the Sun across the heavens, the moon through her phases, and the seasons of the earth's fertility.

The sun was honoured because of its obvious and vital life-sustaining warmth and light – without it everything would die. The sun appeared constant in its cycle, but how could you be sure? It may not have been so unless rituals were religiously performed to keep it alive, to keep it turning, and call it back from the darkness each day and each year.

The moon was honoured because her cycles were so evident, and being changeable she was seen as responsible for everything that moves in cycles – the fertility seasons of women and of the earth.

Funeral dance, Wall painting, Etruscan 4th Century BC.

And the earth, Mother Earth, must be honoured, cared for and encouraged in her cycle so that she continues to be fertile and provide food for her children, so that the Crone of the Underworld transforms into the Maiden of Spring and then into the Mother of the Harvest.

Under the wheel of the heavens and the turning of the seasons our life too is a cycle, from birth/beginning to death/ending, and on and on. Seed in the womb, seed in the earth; tender shoot, tiny babe; growing to maturity, growing to fruition; and then the release of the fruit and the return of the form and the seed to the earth, to the ground of being, to the source of life. We are a circle within a circle with no beginning and never ending.

Narrowing the lens, we have the cycle of day and night flowing ceaselessly into and out of each other; narrowing it further and there is the breath, the energy of the life force; it too is cyclic, and mirrors the

greater cycles with the rhythm of expansion and contraction, of rising and falling, becoming and dissolving.

Our ancestors, observing nature, saw how, for example, the movements of the moon influence many natural phenomena such as the tides, birth, the menstrual cycle. They saw their lives as cycles within cycles and echoed the circle of the earth and sun and moon in their round houses and their round dances. They understood their place in the scheme of things so, naturally, they danced in a circle, and when the circle was open, as in many Greek dances, it still moved in circular form, with a leader to channel the group energy.

The famous specialist in traditional dance, Philip Thornton[1], who first brought Balkan dance to Britain and laid the foundation for the present repertoire of Balkan dances enjoyed in the folk dance and Sacred/Circle Dance world, describes in his book *'Dead Puppets Dance'* an experience he had in Albania of dance as ritual.

He watched two circles at night dancing around a small fire of aromatic wood; twelve women in the inner circle, twelve men in the outer. The circles were moving in opposite directions with completely different steps to the accompaniment of a drum. They were dancing the seasons, the twelve months of the year dancing around the sun/fire. When the rhythm changed and became slow and measured the men moved back becoming the outer circle, and the women danced slowly bowing to the fire while the men stood still on the spot.

Then with great shouts the two circles somehow became one, the rhythm speeded up and the dancers danced fast and furiously in and out towards and away from the fire, gradually getting closer and closer, until with another great shout they all jumped into the fire and stamped it out; the sun had died and it was winter once more!

Gradually the intellect took over from the intuition, invention replaced observation, and science gave us facts. If you have a watch you pretty soon stop relying on the position of the sun in the sky to place you in the daily cycle. Before long you don't even notice and time marches along in linear fashion on your digital watch or clock, divorcing you even further from the experience of circle reality. If you are given a scientific explanation for why spring always follows winter you lose the need to invoke and work with the natural forces such as the sun and moon. If you fall sick and a quick visit to the doctor or a pill or two from the chemist give relief you soon lose the need to observe the natural healers growing around you on the earth.

We began to hand over the sovereignty of our lives to the experts, the professionals; we bought the myth that mind knows better than matter (alias mater, alias the 'Mother principle' manifest in the natural world). The line overtook the circle, time subjugated instinct, and we were on the slippery slope to the disconnected, frantic, materialistic world of the 21st century, the world of the quick fix and the rush from past to future which overlooks the moment of 'Now' when life happens.

This descent into dissolution of the circle has however been a necessary stage of our journey towards self-knowledge and awakening. The baby has no sense of its separateness, it will only gradually realise that the smiles it is used to seeing up above are not a part of itself, whereas the object waving in front of its face and occasionally landing **on** it, **is** a part of itself. We originated in a dream state, existed in a tribal consciousness knowing ourselves to be part of everything. We felt each other and the plants and animals, with the same intensity as we felt ourselves. Each maiden in the ancient Beltane/May Eve sacred marriage

Round dance, Terracotta, Boeotian, 6th Century BC.

rites in the Avebury henge in Wiltshire felt herself to be a spring flower, to be the awakened earth, and each youth a shaft of the sun. They understood, not through the intellect but instinctively, that through their coupling they were uniting earth and sun and that their dance in the ritual ecstasy was for the creation of life in the womb of the earth as well as in the human womb.

But we lost this dream state of oneness with all that is: we left the Garden of Eden and began the lonely trail down into individuation. We did this in order to understand who we are. The baby slowly realises it is a separate being and eventually understands that it can run its own life, and make choices about how to relate. We became isolated individuals so we could see the whole, each other, and ourselves clearly and make a clear informed conscious decision – to return, or not.

We **are** returning to the Garden but now we know, now we are aware! We have eaten of the tree of knowledge and we are able to take responsibility, knowingly, for ourselves. We re-create this truth in Sacred/Circle Dance. Sacred/Circle Dance brings individuals back into the circle consciousness. It reconnects us with a moving whole, fragments at last reunited, cells in one corporate body, the split healed.

As the line replaced the circle so the dance form changed: from something that was a community happening it progressed into straight lines, squares, to couples, then to individuals dancing alone. In the rock scene today everyone dances alone, mostly unrelated, and without the sense of connection, of being part of a whole. In Break Dancing even different parts of the one body dance on their own! There is no further it can go on the road of fragmentation, the limit has been reached and inevitably – although the predominant dance form is still individuals or couples – the upward curve is happening, disintegrated parts are becoming again integrated, and the circle is returning.

> *'We are dancing on the brink of our little world of which we know so little: we are dancing the dance of life, of death; dancing the moon up in celebration of dimly remembered connections with our ancestors; dancing to keep the cold and darkness of a nuclear winter from chilling our bones; dancing on the brink of ecological awareness; dancing for the sake of dancing without analysing, without rationalising and articulating; without consciously probing for meaning but allowing meaning in being to emerge into our living space.'*
>
> *Deep Ecology. Living as if Nature Mattered.*
> Bill Devall

6

Findhorn Revisited
– I go deeper in

| *'Ask Terpsichore!'* |

In the 12 months following my initiation at Findhorn, I attended all the three Sacred Dance week-long courses that were on offer there, and finally the three-week training course for would-be teachers. The week-long courses were blissful experiences for me. I felt I had at last found my slot in life and a true 'family'. I anticipated the training course would take me to the depths of the Dance as the week courses had taken me to the heights but I was to be disappointed.

It was fun but I was ready and hungry to know what it was all about, what lay behind, what was really going on when we danced, I wanted to learn about energies and symbolism. I knew there was more and I wasn't getting it by simply repeating dances over and over again.[*]

I had noticed a man on the periphery of Findhorn and of the Dance, moving like a shadow around the circles but never being directly involved; there was something about him, about his bearing and his contained and intense energy that intrigued me. I intuitively felt that he knew what I wanted to know, and one afternoon I located his caravan, and knocked on his door, found out his name was Keith and prepared to 'sit at the feet' and be instructed in the mystery.

He was silent for quite a while after I poured out my yearning, and finally when he replied all he gave me was two words – *'Ask Terpsichore!'*[2]. I wanted to say – *'Is that all?'* It **was**! Great! I had expected information, facts, brilliant esoteric concepts, I wanted him to hand it all to me there and then, and all he did was tell me to take my request

---

[*] I believe the current training at Findhorn is very different.

25

elsewhere, to Terpsichore, the Greek muse of the Dance! I felt like weeping in frustration and disappointment! That reaction lasted all of thirty seconds and then the truth kicked in! I didn't like it, I still wanted him to do it for me, but his answer did give me everything I needed!

He was saying don't go on looking outside yourself for the authority – which had always been one of my major blocks – you can receive it directly. No Gurus, follow your own knowing, your own inspiration, your inner creative muse, your direct link with the Cosmic Dancer and the Great Circle. He could have told me what he knew, but it wouldn't have been **my** knowing! It was one of the most empowering experiences of my life, a key that unlocked the door to intuition and creativity, a free pass for life to the Reality behind the reality.

On the practical level there was one frustrating aspect to an otherwise magical dancing time at Findhorn. We thoroughly learnt and danced a cassette tape full of dances during each of the Sacred Dance weeks, but were not allowed to buy a tape of the music! So much for my vision of this wonderful Dance spreading everywhere! Copyright law was said to be the reason, (which may have had some truth in it but mostly the music was folk music from countries on the edge of sophisticated Europe and all but impossible to trace).

It felt totally unreasonable to me – the Dance didn't belong to Findhorn or to anyone, any more than the sun did, and people were aching to learn and share these dances. Oh, the anguish and the helpless fury to leave for home with a week's dances vibrant in my body and not to be able to pass them on.

It was David Roberts – one of that original group which learnt the dances from Bernhard – who by-passed the Findhorn ban and started producing 'pirate' cassettes. He, along with Janet Scott and Errol Wiener, brought the Dance down to England. The sluice gates were open and the Dance wave poured out!

Image of Terpsichore, Greek muse of dance.

7

Expansion
– of the Dance network

'It is not surprising that the circle has been part of rituals that attempt to involve, channel, contain or invite experiences of the sacred.'

'Creating Mandalas'
Susanne E. Fincher

I remember David Roberts, at the beginning, warning the handful of the then teachers that Sacred Dance would grow to be huge, and wondering if we would be ready! I took this to mean that we had a lot of work ahead of us in order to keep up with, or better still ahead of, the escalation. Work in practical ways such as quality music tapes (which meant checking sources), networking (sharing information and supporting each other), suitable venues, comprehensive and sensitive publicity etc. but also personal work – we needed to be ready with effective teaching skills, physically fit to run the many weekly groups we were soon to be faced with, and we needed to be fine tuned as conduits for the Dance; this meant clearing up ego issues, freeing up personality hang-ups and aligning ourselves constantly with the Source and the higher will. In other words, it was time to become professionals!

In 1984 Colin Harrison drew up a list of seven aims or guidelines for a Sacred Dance network to support the teachers and promote the Dance: to draw up a list of all teachers and groups to be publicised in a newsletter; to arrange and advertise meetings and workshops for the exchange of information about dances and ideas to expand; to send out a diary of events; to circulate and improve music tapes; to find music and words for the dances and to list the musicians; and lastly to set up a forum for ideas to take the Dance forward. Rosa James (then Rosie) heard the call and sent out a single, hand-written, A4 sheet with a list of teachers and groups. This was the first newsletter, which grew into

27

Grapevine[3], the current professional businesslike quarterly network journal.

A neat system of annotation was devised so that the dances could be recorded and handed on correctly and succinctly. A code indicated the direction of the dance; the direction of the nose (when it's not the same as the body); whether the step is to a long beat or a short one; which foot moves – R or L – and what it does, e.g. goes forward – F, steps sideways – S, hops – H etc. This method gives an accurate and complete picture of a dance almost at a glance, though some people prefer to have it all written longhand. Different brains, different ways of learning! It's a sign of health in any organisation when diversity and differences are embraced.

Then in November 1984, as the demand for the music for the dances grew, a guideline for music distribution was drawn up. This was to address some growing concerns about copyright. Dishonouring the sources and musicians and indiscriminate distribution of the music, undermined the integrity, and authenticity of the dances.

1. Tapes (it was tapes or tapes in those far-off days!) will only be sold to workshop or class participants. Preferably to be included in the class price.
2. Each tape to be clearly marked:
   For educational purposes only.
   Not for public sale.
3. No price to be included on the tape.
4. A percentage of the selling price to be donated to a musicians' charity of each teacher's choice – and records and receipts to be kept of each donation.
5. 'Master' tapes to be kept under control and not to be given out willy nilly to everyone, and only in agreement with these guidelines.
6. Quality to be consistently improved. Care to be taken not to sell an inferior product other than at a low price.
7. Owners of copyright – where and if possible – to be gradually tracked down and negotiated with.

The network was learning professionalism! This marked an important development, one that by-passed some of the other new movements on the 'alternative' circuit. Unless we were grounded, the Dance would float around for a while and then 'poof!' expire like a soap bubble. What this development signified was that the Dance was truly being grounded, that the right and left hemispheres were working together, that we were not airy-fairy space cadets floating two feet above the ground, but responsible serious adults working practically as well as creatively with the world of Sacred/Circle Dance. It was imperative, as David Roberts said, not to throw the baby out with the bath water, but to bring the best of the qualities of the Piscean age into the Aquarian arena. If we were to be successful in the task of bringing this precious gift of the Dance to as many people as possible we had to anchor the dream in the practical world, we had to bring spirit and matter together.

Before too long there were even a few, a very few, who took professionalism seriously in the sense of earning a living from teaching Sacred/Circle Dance. But that's jumping ahead.

The evolvement of the Dance resembles a rose unfolding. I choose the metaphor of a rose for its connection with the Feminine, with the heart, with love, which the circle embodies. This expansion was all divinely orchestrated. We started with short two hour sessions of dancing, and each new stage of expansion arrived at precisely the right time: you could say it was a case of 'when the teacher's ready the event arrives!' So as teachers felt empowered to expand what they were doing Dance 'workshops' started to happen in addition to the 2 hour sessions.

- Gradually we were ready to run half-day events, then full days, then whole weekends!
- Then came the first Sacred/Circle Dance Camp Weekend – in 1985 in the Welsh hills. There were barely twenty of us including 'live' musicians! It was a very earthy event as the property was suffering a 'plumbing' crisis due to the severe drought, and one of the regular dances was in to the bushes carrying a trowel!
- A group of singers and musicians came together to produce two tapes of music for basic dances, and the Dancing Circles music distribution business was born.

It was all heady stuff but not too heady to handle if the work of personal development and release went alongside. The entire evolvement of this beautiful Sacred/Circle Dance Rose was, and is, being choreographed from a higher level. Each stage is monitored and a new strand only arrives when everything is ready for it.

Findhorn was the marital bed of the Dance! It was where the union between the old Folk dances of Europe and the new Aquarian energy was consummated. The offspring that was birthed was nurtured and fed with love but when the growing fledging was ready and eager to fly there was a reluctance to let it go.

29

One of the main pioneers in the 'Free the Dance' movement was Colin Harrison. He it was who changed its name to 'Circle Dance' in his application for an Enterprise Allowance, feeling that '*Circle* Dance' would be a more likely candidate for a grant than '*Sacred* Dance'. He got the grant and the name stuck. It seemed a good move because it would help the Dance spread and because there were other traditions who also danced their own Sacred Dance; there were those too who felt they had ownership rights to things sacred. Sometime in the first couple of years of my involvement with the Dance (so before the name was changed in England to Circle Dance) I was challenged by a Tai Chi teacher in the West Country to explain why the Dance was called Sacred. I did my best! He was asking, he said, because he was involved in the Nine Ways of Zikr which was considered a sacred dance in the Muslim tradition, and there are other traditions, he said, also doing their 'sacred dance'! No one had patented 'Circle Dance' and it didn't step on any other dancing toes.

At the time I liked the idea of letting people discover the sacred for themselves, but after a while I came to feel that something vital had been lost with the change. Maybe it was my North Country upbringing where a spade was called a spade, but eventually I felt it was time to 'tell it how it is' and stop compromising with 'out there'. So I started calling it Sacred/ Circle Dance, which sounded a bit like a compromise too, but did seem to say it all! Dancing up in the north around this time, the name thing came up in conversation with the woman who was organising the event and she loudly and clearly informed me that she could have got at least twice as many people if it had been called 'sacred'!

As, on its own, the name 'Circle Dance' doesn't convey the spiritual element and as circles may form with either a light or a dark intent, I opted for 'Sacred/Circle Dance' which I felt does tell it how it is – the dance of the sacred circle of life. I like the present way of putting a '/' between the words 'Sacred' and 'Circle', so honouring all three prefer- ences – Sacred Dance, Circle Dance **and** Sacred/Circle Dance!

The expansion of the Dance mirrored my own involvement with it. Gradually I gave more and more of myself to it and gradually felt stiff places within me softening and my connection with my inner joy growing. Three years after the Dance had exploded into my life and begun the process of exploding my life, I was out of my marriage, home- less, sleeping on various friends' floors but following the thread of the Dance.

It was possible at that time in Britain – mid 1980s – to apply for a grant to set up your own business. It was called the Enterprise Allowance and gave you, if you met the requirements, £40 a week for a year. Looked at cynically it was probably a way to bring down vote-unfriendly unemployment figures, but whatever the motive, it was a god (or maybe – a goddess) send! Following Colin Harrison's example I applied for it, got it, and joined the 'professional' Sacred/Circle Dance teachers – Anna Barton, David Roberts, Michael Loxton and Colin – thus swelling their numbers by 25%. Even today there are only a handful of teachers who earn their living this way.

At around the same time as the Dance found me, I experienced a 'calling'. When 'She' first came to me I was overcome with emotion because she was so familiar! I remembered her! Never had such a thing happened to me, at least not since seeing the fairies as a very small child! I was awestruck at being able to 'see' and 'hear' a spirit being, an angel being, and to feel that this beautiful lady holding white lilies was calling me was simply the most wonderful thing that had ever happened. There and then I dedicated myself to her service, giving myself to her to help in her work in whatever way she needed.

Who exactly She is I don't know and I don't need to know, it doesn't matter to me. I call her 'The Lady', and I know I serve her through the Dance. What I understood then was that I would work for Her through the Dance and that the Dance would support me, and so it has – unfailingly. Since that moment I have been sustained in every way by the Dance for twenty years.

8

S.E.E.D. – Sacred Earth Energy Dance
– how the Dance affects planet earth

'We have not forgotten the Old Ways.
How could I say that I do not know how to dance
We still know how to dance
We have forgotten nothing.
We know how to call the rain
If it rains too hard we know how to stop it
We call the summer
We know how to bless the world and make it flourish.'

Kogi Indians of Columbia

As the circle of the Dance grew, it touched and flowed into many other circles. People began weaving the Dance into whatever they were already involved in and found it enriched what they were doing. Thus the Dance was woven in with education, taken into schools and prisons and adapted for special needs groups for children and adults with learning or physical difficulties; Dance and Astrology wedded together; Dance and story-telling, Dance and Yoga, to mention but a few. My own special interest was the cycle of the year, the nature kingdoms and the seasons and their festivals.

The Prophecies of the Hopi Indians had predicted that the year 1986 would bring the activation of all earth's sacred sites, and sometime during that Spring I felt a calling, an inner compulsion, to help with this. On my travels to dance in various parts of the country in the early months of that year, I was to meet one person after another expressing the same urge – to get out on the land, to the special places near them, the 'sacred sites', and DANCE!

Travelling is frequently a creative time for me. I may get the steps for a dance, or a flash of understanding or inspiration. On one particular car journey up to Yorkshire that April, sitting quietly on my own in the back, a beautiful 'divine' idea popped in. The synchronicity of so many people with the same compulsion to dance on their sacred earth needed listening to. I felt that 'The Lady' was sending this impulse rippling simultaneously through many people to awaken the earth through activating her power points – the high places, stone circles, sleeping 'dragons' etc. – by sacred dancing and intent. So the 'divine idea' was – what if circles across the country, across the world, were co-ordinated to dance at each of the eight turning points of the year! And what if they danced the same dance, one that held the energy of that particular festival! And what if the energy built up by this were to be directed to some particular place on the earth at a specific time - what a network of light that would create!

I sent an exploratory letter to the people leading Sacred/Circle Dance in Britain, Europe, Canada, the States and Australia. The response was without exception supportive and enthusiastic and so at Beltane 1986 we were off, and the S.E.E.D. – 'Sacred Earth Energy Dance' – network was formed! The project was initiated with a dance from the island of Kos, **Enas Mythos**, a Greek 'greetings' dance, to greet each other and the earth, and the energy was focused on three stone circles in Cornwall – the Hurlers near Liskeard – and radiating from there across Britain and down into France.

From this small beginning with a handful of committed Dance teachers, the network grew organically. At its peak I was sending out between 80 and 90 newsletters, the majority in Britain, the rest to Europe (France, Germany, Sweden) and to US, Canada and Australia. As well as the groups, there were many individuals, committed to healing the earth in whatever way they could, who joined, dancing on their own if no circle were available!

The dances were varied in style and place of origin, each relevant in meaning, energy, and symbolism to its festival. Many of the circle dances in our repertoire relate to the old rituals for growing crops and sacrificing animals. So there was a body of dances tailor-made to fit some of the festivals. There are dances to encourage the grain to grow tall, to invoke the return of the sun, to bring rain, to prepare the earth for sowing, to celebrate the harvest and so on.

Two of the focus points showed up twice in the eight years – Glastonbury town (Imbolc 1987) *and* Glastonbury Tor (Beltane 1990) (maybe acknowledging the parallel universes that exist in that town!), and the

Dancing at Glastonbury Abbey, Glastonbury Dance Festival 2002. Photo by Esbjorn Aneer.

Kremlin in Moscow also called for attention twice – Lammas/Lughnasadh 1990 and again at Beltane the following year! There was only one dance though that turned up twice, **Adjon Az Isten** from Hungary, first for Yule 1990 with the focus of Budapest, and then two years later at Samhain focusing on a place in Bulgaria. Why? Who knows? Someone certainly, but it wasn't conscious me!

The process of selecting the dances and the focus was as varied as the dances themselves. More often that not I had an instinctual knowing and a dance would just 'pop in'. This is the way I have always 'chosen' the dances for any dance event and still do. I suppose a more accurate way to describe it would be – the dances select themselves! I find myself humming the music for a dance, or the name is suddenly there on my mental 'screen'. Sometimes they tumble over each other 'Me, me, ME' in their enthusiasm to be noticed and chosen! For they too are 'beings'.

Occasionally there was no obvious reason why a particular dance turned up; it was only as the time of the festival came close and I danced it that it became clear. Even then it was often beyond conscious understanding, but more of an 'Ah hah!' feeling inside.

Sometimes the reason for a focus would be clear at once; it was obvious why for example the source of the River Thames would come up for Imbolc 1992 – the time of the cycle concerned with thawing and flowing, or why for Samhain 1989 – the crack between worlds – we danced for the San Andreas fault. Then sometimes, during the time between writing the newsletter and dancing the dance, events occurred that made the focus clear – maybe a political situation or a natural disaster in the area that called for healing, but frequently the reason remained a mystery. Why for instance were we tuning into the Blue Mosque in Istanbul at Eostre/Spring Equinox 1988 or an obscure region in the Bulgarian mountains at Samhain 1992? This was 'Angels-at-Work', some weaving of energies, and some rebalancing of earth's meridians that was not our concern. We raised the energy; 'they' made use of it. And I do mean 'angels'! There was an energy Circle directing this operation, we were simply the necessary earth link in a vast and subtle manoeuvre.

In spring 1994 it came to an end with the Eostre letter. Quite suddenly I knew it was done and the cycle was complete – eight years of eight festivals.

A few years later I travelled the wheel of the year one more time, researching further and updating my experience of the festivals and finally brought it all together into book form. This, *'The Sacred Earth Energy Dance Book'*, is available as a self-publication.

9

Inner and Outer
– the vertical and horizontal axis

'*Past and future veil God from our sight*'.

Rumi

'*The more you are focused on time – past and future – the more you miss the Now, the most precious thing there is . . . the only thing. It's all there is.*'

Eckhart Tolle

Let's now begin to look at what lies behind the steps, starting with the basic energy alignment in Sacred/Circle Dance.

The starting point is the inner centre. The impulse for the Dance comes from the centre of gravity within the body and from the central axis. This is where we start. The Dance moves from this centre and out; although the learning of the steps happens from the outside in we dance out **from** this centre. The dancer moves always from the strength of her or his centre and the vertical axis running through the body.

Bernhard Wosien saw the deep or high spiritual significance of Classical Ballet and developed what he called a *Meditation on the Cross* based on the ballet positions.

In first position the feet are turned out with the heels together and the arms curved in front with fingers touching at the solar plexus. The dancer is alone and centred, but at the same time poised and ready. Bernhard called this position *The Apprentice*.

In the second the feet are shoulder width apart with the arms out to the sides. This signifies an opening and a readiness to connect with others. This he called *The Journeyman*.

In the third position the feet are at right angles with the right heel touching the left instep; the right arm is curved up above head and the

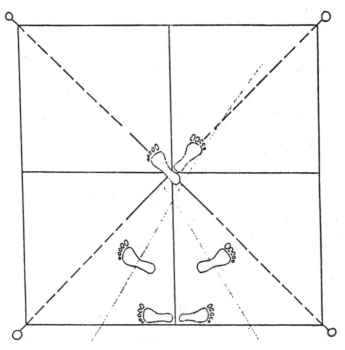

Diagram of the first three ballet positions. Sketch by Bernhard Wosien by kind permission of Maria-Gabriele Wosien.

left out to the side. This is the ready-to-serve position, the stance of Hermes the messenger of the gods, who spirals energy up and down through the body, connecting heaven and earth. This is *The Master,* who knows himself and can dance at the centre of the circle.

Fourth position he saw as a variation of second, and fifth a variation of third.

Following Bernhard, in the courses I run training people to teach the Dance, I teach a routine using the first three positions followed by my own addition which works with the static and diagonal crosses. This discipline bring these alignments strongly into the body to create an empowering energy structure and if used regularly it greatly helps focus, posture and centredness in everyday life.

So the dancer moves out from the inner containment of first position and opens into second position, stepping from the vertical on to the horizontal plane, and indicating that the dancer is ready to begin the journey.

On every journey it's a good idea to know where we're heading yet the only part of the journey that is real is the present step, the one we are taking at the moment! A journey of 1000 miles always starts with the first step; one step is all that's needed to get going and one step is all that's needed to **keep** going. Both an outer and an inner purpose for the journey are necessary. No one makes a journey without an outer purpose even if it's just to 'follow your nose'. Usually the outer purpose is to reach the destination! An inner purpose could, for example, be to release attachment to an old unhelpful relationship or to move in an unfamiliar space to allow something new to come in.

Paradoxically, a spiritual inner purpose for an outer journey is about not moving anywhere; it is about staying in the present moment and in the consciousness of the one particular step that is happening now, with no regard to where it may be leading in the future, not even in the next second. It is possible however for silence and sound, movement and stillness to exist simultaneously, and when we dance, outer and inner purposes are combined: there is movement towards, **and** there is inner stillness in the moment of Now.

We see this union in the shape of the equal-armed cross, which aligns, horizontally, with time and with the movement both away from and towards; and, vertically, with the deepening awareness of the Being, of timelessness, of the Now. Bernhard Wosien related the vertical axis to space and the horizontal axis to time. I have come to prefer them the other way round – seeing time as movement, relating therefore to the horizontal, and seeing the infinity of timelessness, or the eternal Now, as relating to the vertical. Both pictures have meaning.

Life, everyday life, mostly happens on the horizontal plane; we rush through time, from somewhere, towards somewhere. But as Meister Eckhart, the 13th century spiritual teacher, says: '*Time is what keeps the light from reaching us.*'

Except for a very few enlightened beings, people are in transit from the past to the future, always moving towards some goal, some objective, missing the wholeness of the moment. For the majority of people life is about 'doing'; even an aim or a desire is a thought, and a thought is something that's **done**. As everyone is so busy coming from the past towards something in the future, the present, in which both past and future happen, is overlooked – except when something happens suddenly and brings a jolt of awareness.

In the winter of 1993 I had one of these wake-up jolts. On the day before the solstice, I was determined that my elder daughter, who had come back to live with me, should have a great Christmas and at the last moment decided to take her away. I booked a crazily priced self-catering cottage, which entailed a round of frantic shopping, packing and exhausted panic. Finally we were on the road, but far too late according to my intended schedule! Looking back at the 'me' in that car it's absolutely no surprise that I crashed. Energetically I was already in Devon, settling into the cottage, nursing my daughter (fresh and pained from a heavily impacted wisdom tooth operation) probably even cooking the Christmas lunch. Certainly I wasn't, in any but a superficial physical sense, in that car driving down a wet A (main) road in the sleet.

It was a violent way to be brought into the body, into the moment, into the 'vertical', but it worked. Having agendas ripped away like this is a harsh but effective way to learn both to flow and to be in the present. Christmas was spent in our beds in my rented top flat and it was exactly what we both needed. Physically I was only bruised, but I felt quite literally shattered, and that is in fact what had happened – the structure of my life with all its tension and straight lines ahead had been shattered.

I had been racing along on the horizontal axis and been brutally aligned on the vertical, and the enforced retreat allowed me the space to 'get it', to listen to the vertical axis, and eventually this allowed the fragments to re-group in a different pattern that was made not of straight lines but of curves, revolving circles, rising spirals and meandering 'snakes'. I was starting again!

We are each a complete universe operating within a sphere around a central axis. As dancers, we are also, each of us, a pillar of the Dance temple or a pole in the Dance Lodge/Tipi. We stand balanced and firm in our own space; we connect heaven and earth through our bodies so our posture is erect with an awareness that the feet continue down into the earth and the spine stretches up to infinity.

In classical Greek temples the pillars are not at a true 90-degree angle to the floor or ceiling. Each column tilts very slightly in to the centre creating a soaring feel to the building and a sense of fluidity. In the first position in classical ballet the dancer's weight is very slightly forward giving it a minute tilt and bringing it into line with the axis of the earth which inclines towards the Pole Star.

As Bernhard Wosien said *'all of this is not my wisdom, I have it from my teacher, and this tradition of masters goes back in an unbroken line to Pythagoras.'*

It is this tilt that we feel energetically in the Dance Temple alignment before dancing when we atune to the slightly diagonal axis going up to the sun's centre; it is our spiritual connection – focusing upwards and to the centre – whereas our physical destination, our goal ahead, is on the horizontal line.

When there is a strong awareness of the vertical position and of the elevation from the depths of the earth to the centre of the cosmos, the Dance moves out from **within**, rather than being simply a sequence of steps that are taught, and the inner quality of each dance can be experienced and absorbed.

It is the vertical axis that is largely neglected in this current restless society. The vertical axis brings awareness of the present, and is concerned with 'being' rather than 'doing'. The connection the vertical makes is up to the higher reality, and down through the body into the depths of the Being and the depth of the earth. That it connects through the body is most important. It is through the body that the full Being is accessed. This is in part the meaning of Jesus' words to the disciples before the crucifixion, as reported in the apocryphal Acts of St John – '*Whoever does not dance does not know what happens*'.

If circle dances are danced with only the outer purpose, i.e. doing the steps correctly and moving in a physically co-ordinated way together, then what we have is folk dancing. The steps do need to be accurate in Sacred/Circle Dance too, however, because this faithfulness to form releases the essence of the Dance. It is when the consciousness comes in, when there is the awareness of the other dimension, of the state of being in the moment and a sinking into the vertical alignment, that we have *Sacred* Dance. It is these inner and invisible processes that are the source of the joy, the experience of unity, and the magic of the Dance.

The horizontal alignment stretches out beyond us and connects us into an awareness of the rest of humanity and of all the other life forms across the planet, but it is the vertical that connects us into the eternal and infinite Oneness, which we may call God or Great Spirit or Great Mystery, or simply Being. If all that is important is getting the steps right then the inner purpose of the dance is missed; if there is inner awareness, each step can become a deepening into oneself, into essence, and into a relationship, a deep knowing of the precise moment in time, which is in truth all there is. It is as if each step contains all the other steps you have ever taken and those you will take, but also contains the destination, since time is a human construct and all that truly exists is the 'now'. In my everyday life I often feel there's not enough time, but when I dance I experience timelessness and realise how elastic time is, and how, if I focus totally on the dancing, time falls into its proper perspective and I am free of its restrictions.

So what happens in the Dance is a shift from ego/mind-centredness to being-centredness, a resting into the ground of the true Self.

I have frequently wondered over the years why it is – how on earth it *can* be – that someone can turn up for the first time to dance for an evening, fall in love with it, often rapturously, but never be seen again in the circle! I sense that this may be, at least for some, precisely due to this shift into being-centredness. When experienced powerfully for the first time it can be overwhelming. The evening may be relaxing, fun, peaceful, moving, but a lid has been taken off and it may be that what has been revealed is so threatening there is no way the dancer could return at that time for more.

We each know how much reality we can take at one go, and monitor our own awakening. When a door has opened to a new dimension decisions will need to be made about what we do with this. If it cannot be accepted and integrated there will be denial, and the energy that has been released will go into maintaining the pretence that nothing has happened, into cementing the cracks and restoring a normal, familiar, safe reality. However, it is undeniable that something **has** happened! Nothing can ever be quite the same again and it will go on working – regardless of whether it is acknowledged; it will create pain if repressed, or, if faced, an opening to joy and peace and love.

When the mind is quiet then we can know ourselves; there comes a sudden inner stillness that holds intense joy and peace and love within it. Love, peace and joy are not emotions – after all the word comes from the Latin meaning disturbance – but lie much deeper. They are constants, always there, but only come into awareness when there is a pause in the mental stream. This is who we are. This 'revelation' of what lies within, of our true nature may occur during a dance, and in the stillness and silence at the end of the dancing when the circle holds the energy. Joy and peace and love are the natural states of our true being, and the Dance creates the perfect conditions in which to access them.

10

Consciousness and Form
– how to be Human *Beings* rather than Human *Doings*

'That which can be seen has no form and that which cannot be seen has form.'

Hariashingyo, the Buddhist wisdom and heart sutra

Are we, as Joseph Campbell asks, the *'vehicle of consciousness'* or are we *'the consciousness'*? *'Is this body the vehicle of light or is it the light?'* Present day consciousness is so tied up with the form it has created that the form is frequently taken to be all there is.

Sacred/Circle Dance combines form and consciousness. It takes us through the one to the other. Through the transient form of the dances we move into the realm of pure consciousness, which is everlasting and through which we are one with all beings. We learn the form of a dance – the steps and movements and style – and practise these until they are automatic. When our bodies know the steps and are free to move without conscious thought and direction then the meaning and energy encoded within the dance can come through. The mind having performed its function can be given time off and pure consciousness can dance us. We are no longer **doing** the steps, no longer **doing** the act of dancing but have transcended form and the Dance is dancing us. Then our spirit, our soul, our essence, our Being, is where our body is and we are 'home', knowing, for the duration of that dance, or maybe only for a fleeting second in that dance, who we are. We move through the form of a dance, and release the form at the end of it while integrating its inner life, the essence of the dance; we then move on to experience another form and so on and so on; this process teaches us how to be flexible, spontaneous and adaptable in life and gives us a

42

continuous experience of the impermanence of form and the permanence of spirit.

It was said of the famous ballet dancer, Nijinsky, that his body literally disappeared when he danced, and the only thing that remained *'of that muscular being with its strong prominent features are exquisitely fleeting contours, constantly evanescing forms'*.

My training and experience in the professional theatre gave me many gifts. This awareness of mind and no-mind was an important one. I studied my role, learnt the lines – both activities of the mind – but these were only ways to access the essence of the character I was to portray. This study was the mind's job, and only when the learning was complete could there be a letting go of mental energy. Then the creative energy was released and could flow; then there was the possibility of an experience of art, of transcendence.

Not necessarily, however! I could do everything possible to prepare, but the 'spirit' might or might not enter and transcend; this was why the study had to be done and the technique had to be firmly in place – for the times when no inspiration came.

There are moments in the Dance, as in life, when the clouds part and there is a glimpse of ultimate reality, of our divine Self-ness. It is said that humanity can't stand too much reality all at once, which is true; however, dancing with consciousness can open the door that leads beyond form a little wider each time, and each time allowing a little more Reality, a little more of the Essence, a little more of the one who watches from the realm of pure consciousness, to enter.

Another learning from those exciting theatre days was the dual nature of my being. One of the paradoxes of acting is that you have to be immersed in the character, become the character, and yet be aware of what you are doing! In the shuffle and mumble 'Method' acting that originated in US in the 1960s, the aim was Truth, as it is with all genuine artists. Be true to your character and to the situation are great precepts, but it was frequently taken to such extremes that the audience was totally disregarded. It didn't matter if the people in the audience could hear what was being mumbled on stage as long as the actor was being true to the character at that moment! The paradox lies in the fact that it is necessary both to immerse in the character, and to communicate that character to the audience. It is essential to find the balance between being true to your character and being aware of the fact that you are in a theatre and that people have paid money to share the experience of the play you are in.

Without this 'mini director' awareness, the character may be so moved 'it' walks right off the stage and into the front row of the audience.

I realised there were two parts of me in operation on stage – the part that was imbued with the reality of the character, and behind that was this tiny 'director' who was keeping an awareness of that other reality – aware of being an actor on a stage, aware of the furniture, the audience, the subtle differences in energy of each performance etc. Turning this on its head, the one who is immersed in the bigger picture is pure consciousness beyond form, and it is the awareness of form and operating within it that is the job of the 'director'.

This tiny 'director' has taken over the entire 'performance' in the lives of most people today. It chooses the theatre, the other players, writes the script, directs the moves but has no intention of taking a seat in the stalls to watch the show. It has to be up there on stage, controlling every second of the action, constantly correcting and warning and giving notes. This is the thinking, or rather chattering, mind, that if unchecked successfully blocks the door to higher consciousness and to the peace of the Being.

The Dance is a perfect medium for the 'director' and the 'performer' to be integrated. Once the form is integrated – i.e. the steps and style of the dance have been absorbed – you can hand over the director's role to the circle. By the act of holding hands and becoming linked in a circle, you know there is no way you can step off the edge of the 'stage', so the 'controller' is not needed. I often see people coming to dance for the first time who are nervous of the unknown, of what might be asked of them, of making a fool of themselves, and what a joy it is to see them relax as they gradually realise they can give their 'director' the evening off, or rather that they can take their 'director' dancing too! What a sense of relief to be free, to be so in the body at last.

Once the 'director' is absorbed into the Dance, the dancer is free to totally Be in the Dance, to let go through the rhythm and the music and the repetition of the movements into the wondrous depths and heights of the Being, which is the realm of pure consciousness. You 'bliss out'! You dance yourself into 'heaven'! Of course heaven is where we are all the time, but that's the problem – that **'time'** word! Time and its administrator, the mind, may have been in the way but the Dance opens up the possibility to experience that limitless joy of Being.

11

Symbols and Shapes found in the Dance

'If we were sure of the meanings we would not need the dance.'

Dorothy Bryant

In recent years I have noticed a shift in the consciousness of the people who dance. It used to be enough just to dance, now there is a hunger for more. Initially I was extremely reluctant to talk about what I perceived was happening during a certain dance or what a step might mean, or even to mention energy. Reluctant in case it was not what they wanted, and it was only **my** interpretation anyway; reluctant too because there was still a residue of fear in me – with much history! – of being derided for speaking out what I know.

Recently, though, whenever I mention symbolic meanings, or talk about what the energy is up to everyone is alert. Muscles are still, eyes out on stalks, ears pinned back and there is that deep, breathless silence that signifies attention is being fully paid.

As we awaken, the days of acting in blind faith and accepting without understanding are numbered. We have a need now to understand, to know what is happening to us, to be fully conscious. So when we dance there is a desire to know why we dance and to be fully conscious of what is happening when we do. Our whole being – body, feelings, mind, soul, and spirit – has the yearning to be awake and focused.

In Dorothy Bryant's novel *'The kin of Ata are waiting for you'* is this telling passage:

Afterwards I asked Augustine the meaning of the dance.
'It is itself' she said.

45

> *'But movements have meanings. I'm asking you to interpret the meanings of these movements. There must be a great meaning for your people behind these movements'.*
>
> *'Of course the movements have meanings behind them. If we were sure of the meanings we would not need the dance . . . One must dance the dance and go through it to the meaning.'*

The Dance cannot be explained, its meaning cannot be encapsulated in words, it lies beyond the steps, in other words it only becomes ours through dancing, and yet it is useful to have a go at articulating it, at attempting to make the unmanifest manifest in words. It aids full consciousness.

You won't find a manual to explain symbolism in Sacred/Circle Dance, and give you rules to follow. The door will open if you *'Ask Terpsichore – the Muse of the Dance!'* And 'she' will say – *'listen to the dances, **they** are the teachers'*. It will be a subtle teaching, one that is absorbed through the cells of the body, not through the intellect, and it will open and expand as the readiness to be receptive expands.

Symbols are of course relative and can have many meanings; what follows is a combination of my own interpretations and what I have absorbed from Bernhard Wosien and may be keys to open your own knowing.

Dancing circle creating a moving mandala. Photo by Sheryl Ackerman.

Direction of the dance

It has been discovered that there is considerable crossover between the right and left hemispheres of the brain. It is not, as was once believed, a black and white issue of the left-brain being the 'male' side controlling directed action, logical thinking, goal orientation etc. and the right 'female' side dealing with intuition, lateral thinking etc. Maybe it is not just that we now know more about the brain; it **may** be – and there is considerable evidence to support this – that the brain is actually changing, evolving as we evolve, and that the two hemispheres are growing more like each other and closer in function as we come more into balance with our polarities and discover the centre place.

The vast majority of Sacred/Circle Dances moves to the right, anti-clockwise, widdershins, against the direction of the sun. In fairy and folk stories it was necessary to walk three times widdershins round a hill, or special place. North American Indian dances always travel to the left, moving with the sun. This is the way of the old tribal consciousness. It came from the unquestioning acceptance of the unity of life and the human's place within the whole. For reasons of survival the community came first, the individual second.

When we 'fell' from this state of integration and dreamlike oneness we descended the road to individualism and personal responsibility for life choices and decisions. Now, at this point in time, we are consciously choosing to return to the 'garden', so dancing to the right can be seen as returning home, travelling on our way to meet the sun and merge with the Source once again.

The same analogy applies to the way the hands are held – the right palm faces the centre of the circle, or faces up; the left faces back out of the circle. The right palm facing up can be seen as receiving the power of the sun spirit, and the left facing down as passing the energy on into the hand of the neighbour on the left. So 'right' is the direction we are heading and 'left' represents the past, where we have come from. 'Left' symbolises the loss of separate identity and the dissolution of form. The direction of the spiral to the left then is down, into the earth, into the underworld, into the dreamtime; it is the Dionysian place of disintegration, dark rhythm and chaos.

The ancient Greek danced with two gods, two polarity energies – Dionysus on his left and Apollo, the god of the sun, on his right: on the one hand the clear light of reason and directed action, and on the other the forces of the underworld and disintegration. They are polarities but not opposites in the sense of conflicting, rather they are two halves –

both necessary – that together make a whole. The tension they hold implies a unity. Dionysus represents the rhythm in music, Apollo, the time signature, and dancing in the middle and holding the two in balance, is the human, Orpheus, playing the melody.[4] When the time in the music of a society is the strongest element, as for instance baroque, form and reason will rule the age. When the rhythm predominates it signals a break up: pounding drums disintegrating existing structures and values. In the individual, rhythm can be seen as happening in the feet and legs in walking and dancing etc.; time in the head keeping the pattern clear; and the melody as being the song of the heart.

Dancing to the right is our movement through life, and the different kinds of steps we make indicate the various ways we walk on our path through life. We may at times move forward with strength and determination towards a goal; then the first step will be with the right foot indicating left-brain focus and all the steps will have a regular, strong and even beat. With a slow/quick rhythm the slow step gives us time to take stock and to connect with the earth, and there is a feeling of deliberation as if waiting on the slow beat for the right moment before moving forward. Running or skipping or hopping to the right signify the times when the joy of life dances us, when life is easy, we are on track and in the flow of our life.

Moving to the left indicates either a flowing with the intuition, or a time of review. The dance **Between the Worlds** has two very distinct parts; the first moves dynamically to the right with a very strong emphasis on the right foot, the steps are small, making a vertical rather then a horizontal alignment, and the slow beat of the slow/quick/quick rhythm gives us extra time to experience this vertical axis. The second part flows smoothly to the left with big even steps. With the steps to the right we dance firmly and clearly without hesitation through life, while the steps to the left dance **us** flowingly through life, releasing us into the current of instinct and imagination. It's as if in the first section we are using the will to dance upstream against the natural flow, while in the second we are letting the flow take us, allowing the river to dance us.

In many dances we move first to the right – getting on with life – and then take a few steps to the left before continuing. The steps to the left give us a chance to go back where we have come from to review the past, ensure all is finished, lessons learnt and loose ends tied up, before we move again to the right and let the past go. There are times when strong steps going to the right are needed, times when the softer, accepting flow to the left is appropriate, times when life needs challenging and the will harnessing and other times when surrender is what is required.

We need a harmonious balance between these worlds. Dancing such dances facilitates this; it trains and hones both skills and shows us where one side or the other is dominant so we become empowered to dance with conscious balance through life. In a dance such as **Between the Worlds** one dancer may be enraptured with the second part and begin the sequence to the right reluctantly, another may find the steps of the first part quite impossible. Prescription for wholeness is to keep on dancing until both parts are enjoyed equally!

Movement towards the centre represents going to the Source of life, to the centre place between polarities where opposites are reconciled. It relates to the centre in the body where peace resides, the small centre, which, like a seed, holds the essence of the being, a blueprint of the whole, realised Self. There are dances in which the steps to the centre end in an uplifting, a raising of arms, a leg, or both, either in invocation of higher energies or in aspiration. Sometimes there is a bending at the centre of the knee or head or body or all three – in reverence for the earth and her gifts.

Rhythm – the beat and the spaces between

> *'Where heaven and earth meet there is a space wide as a razor's edge or a fly's wing through which one may pass to another world.'*
>
> Upanishads

Rhythm is fundamental to life. In the womb the first awareness was of the rhythmic beat of our mother's heart. We are constantly in rhythm – the rhythm of the pulse, the heart, the lungs, brain waves, sleep and dream patterns, day and night, the pull of the moon towards and away. Moving to rhythm brings us into harmony with the underlying harmony of our bodies, with the harmony of the natural world and with the celestial harmonies. Repetition is the essence of rhythm, and it is the rhythmical repetition of the steps in the dances that calms the nervous system and quietens the mind.

The stage of learning is primarily the job of the left-brain and the frequency pattern of the brain known as Beta. In meditation or sleep the brainwaves change to a deeper Alpha level, possibly deeper still to Theta, and can go even down to Delta, which is close to the resonance of crystals.

The dancers learn a basic sequence of steps: there can be any number in a sequence, though the fewer there are the more effective the meditative effect will be. Two is the minimum number of steps in a rhythm – as, for example, in one of the **Tsamikos**[5] dances of Greece, which has a strong slow/quick rhythm. When the learning is complete it is possible to let go into right-brain dominance and into a deeper frequency pattern – Alpha – and possibly even deeper, until the brain is quiet. Constant repetition, as in a simple rhythmic dance means that eventually the mind has nothing more to do, can let go of the need to control, and can effectively 'go to sleep'; the body is then free to relax into the experience. This has a similar effect to chanting sacred Indian mantras and Taize[6] chants or watching the flow of the waves on the shore, it can induce an altered state, moving us from Beta to Alpha or lower. At these times there is a sinking below the surface mind with its chatter. Dancing the dance for half an hour, an hour, or more, really takes the dancer beyond the little self with its dominating ego that is trying so desperately to be in control, into an experience of the deep still ocean of consciousness and an awareness of the limitless Self.

Different rhythms affect the dancer in different ways, the most obvious being a heart beat rhythm, as in the dance **Breath of Life**.

It both puzzled and intrigued me for years that the majority of dancers found difficulty with the slow/quick/quick rhythm of so many dances – particularly Greek – where a step is taken and then there is a pause before two more regular steps. It is a most powerful rhythm and important for us in modern Western society.

One day – *Eureka!* I got it! I understood why it challenges people; or rather I found an explanation that satisfied me. I saw that this 3 step slow/quick/quick (or quick/quick/slow) sequence in 2/4 time is in fact 4 regular beats divided up into 1/2,3,4. On beat no.2, i.e. the second beat of the first step, there is no step, whereas on the other three there is movement forward; this no.2 beat is the non-step of mystery and power.

There is so much meaning in this 3 step/4 beat sequence; for instance, the four seasons, spring, summer, autumn, and then the dying down into winter, which is the slow beat of the sequence. During the winter part of the yearly cycle, nothing outwardly is happening, the harvest is gathered, the leaves have fallen and the trees are bare, the Green Man has died. But this is the time of the greatest activity of the earth spirit, when her energy is contained within and she is preparing for the eruption of new life in spring. For Hindus this is the season of Kali the Goddess of destruction. Her name means 'black time': the 'black time' out of which all things come and back into which all things go. It is the void, the transcendent, the Mother of all Things.

In present day Western society there is a desperate intent to avoid this descent, to keep everything bright and light, to by-pass or jump over the dark part of the season, drown the night with bright lights, party to avoid the pull to go within and find the bedrock of being.

Society is frantic for amusement, but the Greek origin of 'a-muse' means 'without the Muse'; so amusement is about being cut off from the deep creative wellspring. This I suspect is at the root of the difficulty with this rhythm for our sophisticated Northern selves. There is a pause in the movement when we are asked to not do anything! Horrors! 'Nothing' can be a frightening concept for people who define themselves and find their security through doing. But this letting go step in the sequence of the 3 step/4 beat is crucial, without it there can be no renewal. Winter is when the earth renews herself; winter is when we renew ourselves if we allow the shift from intense outer activity to inner contemplation, assessment and reconnection with the source of life within.

Alan Watts talks of this in *'The Book On The Taboo Against Knowing Who You Are'*:

> *'Hearing melody is hearing the intervals between the tones, even though you may not realise it, and even though these particular intervals are not periods of silence, but 'steps' of varying length between points on the musical scale. These steps or intervals are auditory spaces, as distinct from distance-spaces between bodies, or time-spaces between events.'*

Maria-Gabriele, Bernhard Wosien's daughter, once gave me a special gift. She had come to Stroud in Gloucestershire in the mid-eighties to lead the Easter Sunday in the annual Easter Gathering that Colin Harrison and I had set up. It was a deeply spiritual dancing experience, and at the end, as she was leaving, I thanked her, but she then, to my surprise, thanked me because, she said, *'You understand the spaces between'*.

This space truth is experienced in Hatha Yoga. The asanas, the positions, are only the first part. The asana does the work of stretching and aligning, clearing and opening, but then there comes the relaxation, the 'space between' when what has been done can be completed, when, for instance, the blood that was blocked during the asana can flood through, flushing and revitalising the system.

What is left unsaid is often more powerfully communicated than the spoken words.

Bernhard Wosien, a gifted artist, merely sketched in a limb or a movement, the eye fills in the spaces between making them vibrant and rich with movement and meaning. Implicit, subtle suggestions of violence or sex on stage or in a movie are much more effective than a full-blown graphic exposure of spurting blood, torn off limbs and erotic naked writhing bodies.

Did you ever, as a child, when the delicious freedom of being able to read a whole book alone arrived, prefer not to have illustrations and in fact – as I certainly did – feel resentful at turning the page and seeing someone else's idea of what Captain Nancy or Peter Pan looked like? It never matched and I felt disgusted that I had not been trusted to see the characters for myself. A child is once supposed to have said that she (or he) preferred radio to television because the pictures were better. This may be straying slightly from the path but not in essence, as what I heard in Maria-Gabriele's remark was that it is a gift to value the silence between words, the space between actions because this is where the spirit is free to enter.

The Quakers in their Meeting House services start from this place, and anything that is said comes out of the silence of the spirit and is allowed space to be received within it afterwards. So in the Dance, the stillness and silence at the end of a dance allows the energy to come totally into the body and the being, and allows spirit to re-arrange things or otherwise use what has been received. This, in reality, is where the Dance is, in the spaces between the dances and in the pauses within the dances themselves. It's as if we have sound, speech and music in order to understand and experience silence, as if we dance in order to understand and experience stillness.

It is in the spaces between things that mystery and magic lie. Truly deep communication happens in the silence between the words, the spirit enters in between the words of a prayer; there is peace in the space between breaths, renewed life flowing in the stillness between Hatha Yoga asanas. The act of doing, of acting, prepares the way for the receptivity, for the stillness of being that follows. The hidden step in this sequence, when nothing happens yet everything is happening, is at the heart of the mystery of the Dance. Through it we contact the spirit behind the form, we release the ego and we give ourselves to Life.

Footwork

The Bristol Old Vic Theatre School, where I studied to go on the stage, taught a system of categorising types of people according to the way they move. It was said to derive from the work of Rudolph Laban, a brilliant Austro-Hungarian dancer, choreographer and annotator of dance.[7] Thus there are people with punchy energy, with flicking energy, there are dabbers, flowers, gliders, stampers etc. There are many different ways the foot can be placed when walking or dancing and each expresses a different energy. For example, timid people walk softly, hesitantly, they don't stamp; aggressive people have a heavy tread, they are not likely to glide.

An exercise that I found absorbing and valuable while at the school was simply to observe people moving, noting especially how they placed their feet and then gradually to feel **into** their feet and **into** their shoes. One of the most effective ways to get into a character was to find the walk and the right shoes. A pair of shoes would make me walk in a certain way that made me feel different from myself, and that could, sometimes instantly, give me the person I was to portray. I learnt through this that the way I move affects the way I think and feel!

And vice versa (it works both ways), if I feel depressed I close into myself, my body posture slumps, and my walk is dragging and heavy. If I feel full of joy and optimism, my step is light and has an up–lift and my body soars upwards. If however when I feel depressed and would rather feel joyful, I make the decision to straighten my body and feel it drawn up, my inner self will respond to this body programming. Changing my body posture and my facial expressions changes the way I am.

Dancing feet.

Taking it a step further – **moving** in certain ways influences the inner state even more; if I change from a heavy dragging step and '**do**' a light footed walk, I change from feeling overwhelmed and depressed to feeling light and carefree; if this happens through walking how much more powerful the effect through dancing. Quick light lively steps, skipping or hopping, steps with a toe point or a tap, programme the body and the emotions with joy and optimism; life is not taken too seriously; the outlook is positive, laughter bubbles up from the wellspring of the being. Dances with slow, gentle, even steps reduce the pulse rate and flood the dancer with peace; life is deep, rich and fulfilling and, above all, easy and flowing.

The way the foot touches the ground reveals the energy of the dancer and the relationship of the dancer to the earth. In the Dance there are stamps, glides, taps, hops, brushes and brush/kicks, each has a unique energy that gives a particular message to the body and conveys a different message to the earth.

It is now widely known that the sole of the foot contains a map of the body. One area of the foot relates to the liver, another the kidneys, the head and so on. In this Reflexology system these points are massaged to stimulate or give relief to the corresponding organ. Putting the foot down flat on the ground is therefore about total commitment, about the whole self being present, here I am firmly on the earth! If there is a stamp with it the message is firmer and makes a statement of absolute groundedness and intent. A stamp in ancient warrior dances builds strength and courage and lets the enemy know you are powerful, and this is where you stand and will not be moved. A child stamps its foot to say NO, I WON'T! A mother stamps her foot to say, YES you WILL! You can't stamp half a foot with force – you either stamp or you don't.

There is, however, a step in Israeli dances, which is called a heel stamp, but though it is done with tremendous vigour it doesn't actually stamp, at the last nanosecond the force is pulled up and the heel finally touches the ground softly but with contained power. Beautiful! Strength and gentleness together: controlled power that builds power within! There is also a practical advantage to pulling back on a stamp – it doesn't hurt the dancer! It doesn't jar the spine and the nerves, and there is the extra bonus that it doesn't hurt the earth either!

We talk of '*digging the heels in*', as a mule does when it doesn't feel like moving; it moves its weight back and sits into its heels and that's that! In the eastern meridian system, masculine energy descends, feminine energy rises. Like a roller towel, which is pulled down one side while the other side goes up, the 'male' energy moves down the back of the body, down the hard spine/shield; and the female up the front, up the soft underbelly. So the heels are the end points for this strong linear energy and when the heel is placed the energy comes down the back of the leg and into the earth.

The toes of the foot are 'feminine'; they are only able to touch the ground gently and without weight. Try stamping with your toes! When a dance calls for a foot to point forward the energy rises from the earth travelling from the toes up the front of the body.

In a well-loved Greek/American dance, **Misirlou**, there is a point forward with the left foot with a slight bow of the head. The inclination of the head emphasises the meaning of the toe point – the touching of the dancer's spirit into the earth through the toes, and an implicit reverence for the earth and a commitment to honour and care for her.

I remember observing worshippers in a Shinto temple in Japan: they clapped as they arrived at the temple and I was told it was to summon the spirits, the 'divine' presence. Similarly, a brush or tap with the ball of the foot may signify a calling of the earth spirit. The brushing movement has, too, the feeling of gently massaging the earth, of giving her love.

A Hopi elder – a Grandmother I believe – tells us that a way to heal the earth is for women to dance on her with little brushing steps. Remembering that the sole of the foot contains the energy of the whole person, this signifies a giving to the earth from our whole self.

Lifts

A lift of a foot can mean several things. Men in ancient agricultural rituals leapt high to encourage the grain likewise to grow tall. Many of the old dances from Europe come from this time of unquestioning acceptance of sympathetic magic so a knee lifting high holds the intent that the harvest will prosper. This high lift applies to the men only, the women's lifts are low as if the foot is reluctant to leave the earth; frequently on the women's lifts the foot points down slightly with the toes keeping close to the earth, while for the men the foot is parallel with the earth. For the women there is always an awareness of the magnetic pull of the earth and of women's special relationship and responsibility for the earth, even when the foot leaves it momentarily; whereas for the men there is a sense of uplift, and connection with the sun.

When I first saw Native American women dance at a pow-wow in British Columbia, Canada, I was deeply moved. I felt I understood what it was they were doing. Whereas the men, like gorgeous flamboyant peacocks, leapt and twirled, crouched and pounded till the dust flew, the women held themselves quite still and danced sedately with minimum movement and progressed very slowly. They moved with a simple touch/step and their focus was down and inward. Their intent was to carefully cover every centimetre of the ground. They placed each step so that they connected with every little bit of the path, and with every step the knees relaxed and they sank down into the earth. They were dancing with awareness of their special responsibility as women to care for the earth, for their own tiny piece of it.

Kicks

Kicks are also many and varied. There are kicks where the knee is raised and the leg then lowered swiftly and strongly with foot parallel to the ground but not held just above it as in Greek dance; it's like digging. This speaks to me of subjugation – whereas historically it may have been suppression of an enemy now, for us, it can be subjugation of the ego or of obstacles to our growth. There are loose knee kicks, which feel like a releasing of negativity or of the past. When the knee is flexed the energy is held; when it is loose and the kick ends with a straight leg the energy is free to shoot out of the toes and away. So some kicks are to maintain and build energy – before a battle for example – some are to clear energy out and away.

Hand holds

There are various ways to connect in the circle – the two most common ones are with the arms down, called a *V hold* because the arms make that shape; and a *W hold* with elbows bent and hands slightly in front of body so making a W. The arms in a *W hold* etch a chalice shape, a receptacle, that can be filled with spirit, and the hands connect the dancers on a heart level. The energy stored through a dance with a *W hold* is grounded immediately the arms drop to a *V hold*. There is a definite feeling of the energy of the dance coming down into the body and into the earth when that happens.

Sometimes at the end of a slow dance such as Bernhard's **Sun Meditation**, the arms are raised up high making, as it were, sunrays to channel the power of the spiritual sun, and when slowly lowered this power is brought right down through the body and given to the earth, and the two worlds fuse in the body.

Dances from Armenia frequently have a *'little finger hold'*. Little fingers are interlocked in a *W hold*. Here there is an even stronger connection on the heart level as the heart meridian or energy line runs from the heart down the underside of the arm and into the little finger: we really do give each other our heart with this hold.

Then there is the *shoulder hold* with the hands resting lightly (Bernhard called the arms *'the wings of the soul'*) on the shoulders of the neighbouring dancers. With the upright body and the horizontal arms this creates a static cross, and around this fixed cross the energy spirals up and down the body making the symbol of the Caduceus. Thus spirit and matter come together.

There are *front* and *back basket holds* where the dancers take hold of the hands of the people next but one to them, so the arms are crossed making a dynamic diagonal cross on the fixed vertical of the body, cf. section on 8-pointed star, page 65. The arms weave over and under, hence the basket allusion. In fishermen's dances from the Peleponnese in Greece the crossed arms represent the fishing nets, the dancers are both the fishermen and the fish, and the movement of the steps creates the waves on the sea.

Right/left balance

All movement involves both lobes of the brain. When walking or dancing the left hemisphere is activating the right foot, the right hemisphere the left foot. It frequently happens that newcomers to Sacred/ Circle Dance will announce as they come into the room that they have two left feet! Which, considering this relates to their **right**-brain with its minimal influence on action, seems at first strange; it seems to be saying they have an excess ability to move with awareness! Wouldn't two **right** feet make more sense?

We certainly need both sides of the brain when we dance. The left-brain gets us from point A to point B, from, for instance, the periphery of the circle to the centre; it helps us keep with the group and move in the right direction. Movements directed by the right-brain, however, have sensitivity and feeling: the right will flesh out the bones of the left-brain form with expression.

Is this perhaps what the new dancers mean when they say they have two left feet – that they are unable to bring direction or consciousness to what they **feel,** and is this why they are drawn to this type of dance, sensing it will help them to balance and temper their over dominant right-brain? And indeed it does do that. Similarly those with a strongly

Circle Dancing

1 V hold

2 W hold

3 Little finger hold

4 Shoulder hold

Symbols and Shapes found in the Dance

5 Front basket hold

6 Back basket hold

7 Elbow lock/Fortress hold

8 Teapot hold

Photos by Esbjorn Aneer.

dominant left-brain benefit from the opportunity to experience movement, imagination and changing patterns.

When the two sides of the brain are in balance, the two opposites reconciled and harmonious, fusion happens and the third can be created. In many of the dances the steps move to the right, then to the left and then to the centre; repeating this regularly encourages the balance, the fusion of the two from which the 'third', a new energy, is birthed. We are creating a healing pattern within the body, which gradually and gently brings it back into a state of wholeness.

It is fundamental to life itself that two opposites coming together produce a third. Male and female fusing create a new life from their union. We have seen, in the image of the Caduceus, the twining together of two serpents from opposite directions around a central staff. These two polarity energies in the body spiral up the spine together and meet in the head bringing illumination: the fusion of the two creates a new state of being.

The shape known as a Vesica Pisces is formed by the intersection of two circles so that the circumference of each passes through the centre of the other. Literally it means 'vessel of the fish'. It is a Pythagorean symbol of the meeting of the world of the divine with the world of matter. Pre Christianity it was associated with the goddess Venus and represented the female genitalia, since where the two circles of the Vesica Pisces overlap a new shape is formed, an oval shape, the shape of any number of seeds: also, and most significantly, the vulva. It is symbolic of the gateway both into and out of life.

In this shape we see the trinity of relationships – there is the space that is me, there is the space that is you, and where the two overlap

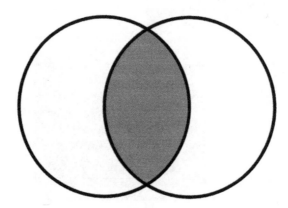

Pattern of Vesica Pisces.

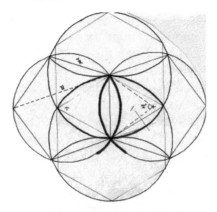

Pattern of Vesica Pisces extends into the Flower of Life.

there is the space that is us. For a healthy relationship all three need to be in balance. If I give too much energy to you, I am neglecting myself and neglecting to build the 'us' part of the trinity, and likewise, if me – my needs and intents – are my overriding priority, both you and the third we create together will suffer.

This balance is implicit in the form of so many of the dances: it is absorbed automatically through dancing in a circle where we have to be responsible not only for our own individual dancing but also for the people whose hands we hold, as well as having a third responsibility for the circle as a whole. It can be seen then how powerfully this kind of dancing can teach balance in relationship.

It is often quite painful to watch a 'two-left-footer' struggling to get a visual or verbal message from their head down to their feet. There's often a lengthy time lag before this happens, and then the feet have to interpret what to do about it, by which time the dance will be well on into the next section. But persevere they mostly do, and it pays off! It is a great joy to watch the frowns of concentration soften and the inner dancer coming to life: to witness the opening up of the old personality paradigms, the belief systems and the conditioned reflexes, and allow the healing energy of the Dance and the circle to work their alchemical magic. People change doing this dancing! They **look** different – younger, softer, more beautiful – because they are contacting who they in fact are, timeless, beautiful beings.

Very occasionally, a new dancer will decide this is not for them. If they give a reason it is usually that they find it too restrictive, they prefer a freer, more individual, self-expression type of dancing. Free dancing may genuinely be what is needed in order to balance up a severely restricted and controlled conditioning or life style; but it may also be that there is a fear of discipline or imposed boundaries, or even a reluctance to take charge of one's life. The challenge that Sacred/Circle Dance offers is to find freedom within form. It is after all the eternal challenge of any society – how do I find my own dance, live the life I want to lead, within the confines and rules and obligations of the community. Sacred/Circle Dance provides an opportunity to experience this balance.

The subtext of such a first time dancer might be something like – *I am an individual with a particular and unique biography, I have values and experiences, which are precious to me. This has been challenged and denigrated throughout my life because my personal truth has been counter to the apparent values and truths of the society. Consequently I close down to protect what I know inside.*

Coming to the Dance, the first thing I am required to do is hold hands with people I don't know and face a circle of unfamiliar people. This is a very scary thing to do – taking the first big step from 'me as an individual', to 'me as a part of something bigger'.

It scares me because of the fear that my personality will be lost, swallowed up in the collective; it scares because of the feeling of being exposed to others as with my arms open and my hands held I can't fold them over my solar plexus as a defence; it's scary to be in a situation where the usual rules of introduction and formalised greeting don't apply, and there is nothing familiar for me to hide behind.

There is much ingrained fear in individuals and society from the centuries of control and repression: fear, basically, that we will not be allowed to be ourselves. That self is then hidden, and often so successfully that it's hidden even from the 'owner'! Personas with uniforms and masks are developed in order to cope with life 'out there', and ensure that inter-action with other people is from behind a clear and safe boundary, and follows accepted rules. It can be extremely threatening to arrive in a situation where the old rules don't apply and where barriers start to feel unnecessary. It **is** a big step to move from a lone place to a community place. The Dance invites that with support and within a safe parameter.

In classical ballet, in what is known as the first position, the feet, as we have seen, are together, heels touching with the toes turned out and the arms curved in front of the body, fingers touching; this represents the individual standing alone complete unto her/himself, the *Apprentice* as Bernhard Wosien named it.

The second position, however, as we have seen, marks a big shift – the feet and arms open out to the sides, signifying a move from solitude, from being one single person, to an awareness of other people, the individual joins the circle; it signifies an expansion into a larger reality, an opening up to others and a willingness for them to come into and be part of your life. When people come into a circle and open their arms to take handhold they are making a decision to be part of something larger than themselves, they are preparing to move from this first, isolated position into the second position. This position is more open and inclusive, but the dancer feels potentially vulnerable. The body is open, the hands are held so the arms are not free to cover and protect the body. The new dancer faces a circle of faces, with no familiar escape route.

I know that things always come at the right time and consciousness moves us where we need to be, and that dead-ends demand alternative routes etc. but I am nevertheless humbled and awe-struck by the courage of people who make this quantum leap; who are prepared to enter an unfamiliar room, face people they don't know, say 'yes' to something they have no experience of, take hands they've never held before and in a split second move from a place of 'me' to 'all of us'!

This opening from first to second position indicates a readiness to move, be it out of a stuck place, out of a restricting life style that no longer works, or simply out of isolation. The repetitive rhythmic movement and music of the Dance together with the accepting and caring energy of the circle melt defences around these restrictive life styles and walls of separateness and isolation, and facilitate a widening and deepening of consciousness beyond the ego box. It is a transforming process.

To take a simplistic metaphor – the process is like baking bread! One grain of dried yeast is limited to being one grain of yeast; a bag of flour only experiences life as a bag of flour, but the yeast and the flour mixed together with water and baked evolve into the miracle of a loaf of bread. It's an alchemical process that turns the base metals of yeast and flour into the gold of nutritional bread.

The Dance is an alchemical process both for the individual dancer and for the circle. The base metals of the lower ego self can be transmuted into the gold of the realised Self, and the base elements of the individual dancers transmuted into the gold of a circle of service. When these elements come together with shared intent there is fertile soil for the spirit to come in and effect transformation, for the 'god' to enter. Of course there is no guarantee he will appear but we can be prepared. As C. Day Lewis says in his poem on sacrifice, 'Final Instructions':

> '*You are called only to make the sacrifice,*
> *Whether or not he enters into it,*
> *Is the god's affair.*'

Harold Hobson, longstanding and highly respected Drama Critic for the *Sunday Times*, talked of the moment of magic that can happen in the theatre, the infrequent moment, which made his job worthwhile. Night after night he would sit through one play after another, some mediocre, some rubbish, some brilliant, but the pure alchemical magic when everything fused and the 'god' entered, he experienced seldom and fleetingly: **that** moment was what it was all about! An actor trains and rehearses endlessly doing everything possible to turn in a good and true performance. That is the craft, but whether it takes off and becomes art is not up to the actor – the actor can't make it happen, all she/he can do is prepare and be ready – that is up to the muse, the genius of theatre, the 'god'.

In all the years I have been doing this Sacred/Circle dancing, the 'god' has never failed to show up. If I do the preparation beforehand for the Dance event and the circle forms, 'he' always arrives, though sometimes, if there has been disruptive energy, or for another unknown reason, not until the last dance, maybe not until the last moment! But come he will!

Symbols, mandalas and labyrinths

Circles

> '*Many religious rituals begin with the establishment of a sacred circle . . . Some ceremonies use circular movement to create an ecstatic state of mind.*'
>
> *Creating Mandalas* Susanne E. Fincher

The circle is a potent symbol for many things. It symbolises the continuation of life, the cycles within cycles and for the feminine in all things. It is the shape of the earth, it is the shape of the moon and the sun, the wheel of life, the circle dance of the seasons. People in harmony with the earth and the natural cycles live, as they always have, in circular dwellings. The square, linear, cornered buildings of today create a barrier between people and nature. Living in a round house, dancing round dances, reconnects us, brings us back into harmony and wholeness.

All the dance forms I have tried have satisfied a physical and emotional need to express myself, but not until Sacred/Circle Dance came into my life did I experience a form of dance that satisfied not just the yearning of my body but also of my soul. Moving in a circle puts the dancer in a more receptive state to things eternal, to the sacred in life.

Susan Fincher, author of *Creating Mandalas*, cites voodoo priestesses, Native American shield makers, Eskimos, Dervishes, and the Plains Indians who all connect to the Divine through the circle in their ceremonies. In the Hymn of Jesus from the gospel Acts of St. John, Jesus leads his disciples in a round dance before the crucifixion so they might understand the mystery.

> *He gathered all of us together and said*
> *Before I am delivered up to them,*
> *Let us sing a hymn to the Father,*
> *And so go forth to that which lieth before us.*
> *He bade us therefore make as it were a ring,*
> *Holding one another's hands,*
> *And himself standing in the midst he said*
> *Answer Amen unto me.*
> *He began then to sing a hymn and to say:*
> *Glory be to thee Father.*
> *And we going about him in a ring answered Amen.*

The circle is a feminine shape. The feminine body – breasts, stomach, buttocks, thighs, and the womb – is rounded, it knows the cycle of moon times through menstruation. Through menstruating and the shedding of the womb each month, and through birthing, the feminine body experiences – in fact, **is** – the circle of living and dying.

The circle is the symbol for all things being equal; in a dancing circle each person is a part of the whole. As the feminine harmonises and draws things together, so does the circle, bringing people together into community.

An increasing number of newly created dances do not have a hand hold, they are danced individually while maintaining the circle form. Dancers then become aware of the energetic form of the circle, which both unites them and gives freedom for each to find their own expression of the form while keeping an awareness of being a part of a greater whole. This is empowering! It is also challenging, as an extra awareness is needed from everyone in order to keep the shape of the circle and monitor the space between dancers. Each dancer learns to hold the energy of the circle form without intruding on each other's space within it.

65

Spirals

In the third position of classical ballet the dancer stands at the centre of the temple where the crosses formed by the intersection of the vertical, horizontal and diagonal axes meet. The dancer is now the Master with feet on the diagonal cross, heel of the right foot against the instep of the left. To do this position properly the whole body forms a spiral which continues on up into the raised arms opening to the light, so the dancer is demonstrating both the axis and the spiral that is forming around it. The combination of axis and spiral shows the threefold principle of creation, maintenance and destruction, or form, growth, and decay.

Spirals are everywhere in nature. A dancing circle is in effect a spiral, since when we move in a circle we can never return to the same point in time. Sacred/Circle Dance awakens the universal power of the spiral form in the dancers and through this form we connect with each other, with all life on the planet, with the earth's depths and with the stars.

Plants, shells, teeth and fingernails, a sunflower head, water eddying, waves folding in on themselves, the galaxies, our bodies' DNA, the hair on the crown of a baby's head, all move in a spiral form. It is as if life itself moves from a centre point and spreads out in a spiral.

Spiral form.

Spirals move in on themselves taking us deep into the centre and into our innermost mystery; they move out from the centre taking us into the world with the knowledge gained from introspection. They bring the whole world in, they take us beyond the little self. Both physical and spiritual energy flow in spirals. Energy is both drawn into the body and sent out from it in a spiral. The Kundalini energy spirals up through the body, moving from basic primal power into pure spirit energy.

In a spiral, as in a labyrinth, there is both positive and negative energy, as there is in stone circles. The negative or reversed energy is in the spaces between the lines and moves in the opposite direction to the line, so in any spiral we have a double spiral.

There are spirals also within the dances; whenever dancers drop hands and turn out and around themselves they create a spiral, moving from a point of origin and opening out. Many dances can be led into a spiral form, indeed some, like the old rhythmic Greek dances, seem to cry out to be taken into a spiral. When a circle dances into a spiral the leader leads the line of dancers on a path of diminishing circles to the centre where the leader then turns, leading the line out again. This means there are two distinct directions of movement happening together in the dance, one travelling its way in, the other travelling in the opposite direction on its way out. It resembles a snake coiling and uncoiling.

This spiral dance is known in folk dance both as the Maze Formula, and also, interestingly, as Kundala, as in Kundalini. The spiral is the basic building block of the labyrinth and many primitive people believe that the soul when it leaves the body at death travels a labyrinth on the way to its destination.

Hurricanes are powerful moving spirals of energy; they swirl and roar but at the centre, the eye, there is complete silence and stillness. At the centre of the circle, at the eye of the hurricane, is a place of utter still-ness and silence surrounded by sound and movement. The sun shines in the still centre of the hurricane while all around is dark swirling chaos.

There has recently been an increase in hurricanes due to the increased number of sun flares. These huge energies move as a vortex across the earth destroying whatever is in their path; what they are doing is sweeping away old energy patterns and imprinting a new energy para-digm on to the earth for her transformation. Sacred/Circle Dance works in the same way; the spiralling dancing circle energy is changing the vibration pattern of the earth and building an etheric web of light, which is lightening the earth. At the same time it is holding the 'eye' at the centre.

67

Lemniscates

A lemniscate is basically a figure of eight lying on its side. This pattern is called the sign of infinity as, like a circle, it is complete in itself and never ending; it continuously loops around and around returning always back to itself. Bees dance this pattern when they return to the hive to give directions to where nectar and pollen is to be found. This form is explicit in some dances where it may be created either by the steps or by the arms; it is implicit in many others, as when a grapevine step travels to the right then back again to the left, forming an elliptical lemniscate. One circle of a lemniscate travels clockwise the other anti-clockwise, flowing into and out of each other endlessly, and dancing this shape connects opposite sides of the brain and brings balance to the body and the personality.

Infinity.

Triangles

Triangles appear in a number of the dances; they are usually formed by travelling towards the centre and out again on a diagonal; the third line of the triangle is then implicit on the circumference of the circle. In a few dances the third line is also formed and the triangle completed. An upward pointing triangle can represent the male energy, rising up to heaven; the downward pointing one, the female energy, the spirit descending into matter, and when the two overlap this makes a six pointed star and symbolises 'As above, so below' as in the Jewish Star of St. David which represents God's rule over the universe in all six directions: north, south, east, west, up and down. The basic step in Balkan Gipsy/Rom dance, the Cocek, is a triangle: the movement is diagonally back out of the circle, then diagonally in again. This forms a downward pointing triangle, ancient symbol for female energy, and this energy is amplified by the constant pelvic movement and hip lifts in this style of dance.

Dancing this shape brings us into the concept of a trinity – be it the Triple Goddess energy of the Maiden, the Mother and the Crone; or Shiva, the Hindu god, with the threefold energy that gives life, maintains life and takes life; or the Father, Son and Holy Spirit in Christianity.

There are the trinities of past, present, future; death, life and re-birth; body, mind and spirit. The trinity also represents the two coming together and creating a third, as in physical birth or in the more subtle energy formed in the space of love between two partners, where the polarities join and create a new form.

Crescents

Many Greek dances are traditionally danced in an open circle, in order, it was believed, either to allow the devil a space to get out, or to allow life energy to enter. In this latter case the lead dancer at the head leaps and twirls in his variations in order to contact this energy and bring it through for his community! A crescent means receptivity, a vessel or chalice to receive divine energy. It also signifies new beginnings as with the new moon. The dance **Moon Meditation** is danced in a crescent, the steps also describe a crescent. The old symbols for male and female were crescents; the male symbol was an upward curving crescent, the female a downward one; they later lost the softness and flow of the crescent when they evolved into two sided triangles.

The Eight Pointed Star

According to Mark Defrates '*The 8 pointed star is a Gnostic symbol, known as the octagram of creation. It is related to Venus, and also sacred to Ishtar. In Nordic traditions the octagram is used to invoke magick and also as a protecting ideogram.*'

Eight pointed star – Mark Defrates Jewellery.

The vertical and horizontal axes form an equal-armed cross. A diagonal cross – the cross of St. Andrew which is seen in the Union Flag from corner to corner – intersects this static cross forming a star with eight points. The body contains this form. Stand straight and you are a vertical axis; open the arms out to the sides and there is the horizontal axis; drop the arms and step out to the side and you form the diagonal axes, which are perfected when the arms are raised. These intersecting lines form what Bernhard Wosien called the *'static and dynamic cross.'* The eight pointed star is associated with dance through this cross that runs through the dancer's body and with music through the eight notes of the octave.

This eight pointed star is also seen in the cycle of the year with the eight stations marking the dance of sun, earth and moon. The fixed arms of the cross are formed by the two solstices – winter and summer; and the two equinoxes – spring and autumn. Between each of these comes a festival marking the seasons of the earth and her cycle of growth and decay. The stations on this cycle are – the seed swelling in the earth, the opening of the flowers, the ripening of the grain, and the composting which feeds the next cycle.

Bernhard Wosien choreographed a sublime meditation dance called **String of Pearls** to Pachelbel's Canon suite in D, which he described as evoking the movement of the planets spinning round the sun. The eight steps of the dance also describe the eight Celtic and Anglo-Saxon festivals of the year, the steps marking each of the eight points of the star within an elliptical circle. On each of the four fixed stations charting the sun's journey – the solstices and equinoxes – the step is a strong 'open' one with the feet apart; on the four festivals of the earth/moon cycle – the earth/fertility cycle between these fixed positions – the feet are crossed so the body is creating a spiral of energy from and to the earth.

Mandalas and Labyrinths

'On the solar celebrations and other religious celebrations, the Celtic adept danced the 'sacred dance' barefoot to absorb the earth's energies through the labyrinth. This was a journey through progressive levels of experience, physical and mental until the vortex at the centre was reached.'

'The Celtic Arts Source Book'
Courtney Davis

A mandala.

A mandala is a sacred symbolic diagram. Mandala is a Sanskrit word, which means 'circle', but it applies both to the centre and the circumference of the circle. Mandalas are used in the Hindu and Buddhist traditions in sacred ritual and as instruments of meditation.

They may be created from precious jewels, flowers, dyed rice, coloured stones, or coloured sand; the sand is made from crushed precious stones. Since each grain of sand is charged with the blessings of the ritual process, the entire sand mandala embodies a vast store of spiritual energy.

Mandalas represent the universe; they are a focal point for universal energy and are believed to be receptacles for divine energy. In meditation and ritual there is a symbolic entering into the mandala and a journey to the centre. The purpose of the journey is to move through disintegration and be made whole once again.

Sacred/Circle Dance is a moving mandala. It can be a simple one with all the dancers in one circle, or more complex with two or three or even more circles, depending on how many dancers there are, one circle within the other. I enjoy playing with the mandala form by having each circle dance different steps to the music, or by 'staggering' the start of the dance, so that the outer circle begins first; the second

71

Seven turn labyrinth.

circle starts after the first dance 'phrase', the third after the next dance 'phrase' and so on. With a dance such as **Prayer to the Light**, which has a walking sequence followed by slowly raising arms on the spot, the outer circle begins and the second starts the dance as the outer begins the arm movements etc. The effect of the rippling arms rising and falling across the circle is like the petals of a rose slowly opening and closing. The more circles there are the more beautiful it becomes.

There are countless mandalas and there are many forms of the labyrinth. All labyrinths are 'unicursal' meaning they have a single path, as opposed to a maze which has many options and dead ends. The path of the labyrinth spirals with many turns and changes of direction; it takes you close to the centre, then, tantalisingly, right away to the outermost path, but inevitably it is gradually drawing you in to the centre and then out again.

The journey to the centre of a labyrinth may symbolise many things: it may be the journey through life, the journey after life through the stars to the next incarnation, a journey through levels of physical and mental experience to reach the spiritual centre, or the journey to the innermost sanctum of oneself, one's spiritual core, or all of them! A labyrinth works similarly to a Native American sweat lodge as a way of disintegrating the ego, dying to old realities and emerging reborn.

One of my favourite dance events is the dancing of a labyrinth. The first time I walked a labyrinth was on a Swedish island. It looked small enough to scoot around in a few minutes, I was certainly not prepared for the journey out of time travelling in to the centre and out again. Coming out I had the strange and strong feeling that I understood everything; not with my mind – the experience had by-passed my conscious mind – but, in my guts, in the cells of my body!

Since that seminal experience I have created many labyrinths and run labyrinth Danceshops (I have come to prefer this word to 'workshops' feeling there is heavy energy around the word and concept of 'work'). Some of the labyrinths were temporary, some are permanent. We have used a variety of materials to make them – white string and metal staples, sand, small stones, twigs and small branches, and easiest of all – certainly to dismantle – whitewash! Labyrinths come in many different patterns and sizes but the pattern I work with is the seven-path labyrinth that is found universally – for instance, in Crete, Italy, China, North America, Sweden. In Britain it is to be seen carved into the rock wall near Tintagel in Cornwall.

As the basic building block of the labyrinth is the spiral there is a strong connection between labyrinths and Sacred/Circle Dance and there are Greek dances in the repertoire that are believed to have originated as Ancient Greek labyrinth dances. According to Plutarch, the Crane Dance was brought to the island of Delos by Theseus after he had killed the Minotaur in Crete. It was danced in a circle around a horned altar and represented the spiralling circles that coil and uncoil in the labyrinth. The first time I danced a Greek dance called **Pogonisios** – which simply means a dance from an area called Pogoni (an area on the Greek/Albanian border) – it was like a *déjà vu*; I shot back in time, feeling I knew that dance from those days in Ancient Greece.

The most magical part of a Labyrinth Danceshop is the Saturday evening when everyone dances individually through the labyrinth by candlelight. On the earth and under the stars (if we're lucky!), the labyrinth lit with candles at each turn of the spiral, at each of the altars to the four directions and along the paths, and with the dancers dressed in white, each absorbed in their own dance, magic is created; it is always a sublimely beautiful and deep experience. Heaven, it seems, comes to earth.

Water

Sacred/Circle Dance and water have a close affinity. Looking at the properties and qualities of water to explore this affinity it's clear that water is similar to Universal Energy: both run through and between all things and through all dimensions, and we depend on both for life. Water balances

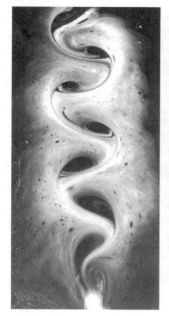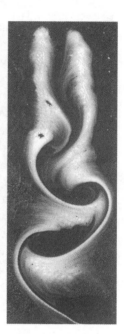

Water flowforms.

energy, as it carries neutral potential and so can balance negative and positive energy.[8]

So in the sense of anti life, 'negative' emotions, 'negative' experiences, 'negative' thoughts, depression, can all be neutralised in the body by water. As our bodies are predominantly made of water – the cells of the brain are composed of 85% water, all other body cells are 75% – water brings the body back into a balanced state. It is a basic life-force energy, which every living thing uses, and so it is a cohesive force bringing things together.[9]

The power of water is greatly increased by intent. Japanese Dr. Masuru Emoto has been researching water worldwide. His book *'The Hidden Messages in Water'* has sold more than half a million copies. Dr. Emoto fills bottles with water from many different locations on the earth – some he exposes to words, music or prayer, others not – he then freezes them and photographs the resulting crystals. Exposure to the energy of anger for instance forms a black hole, to joy a beautiful crystal like a fairy snowflake. What he is demonstrating is that our vibrations and our intent change physical reality. At the heart of intention is the knowledge that everything in the universe is charged and infused, with creative power. It could be said that intention is not something that is **done**; it is something that **exists**, a force, an invisible field of energy in the universe.

In Quantum Physics scientists are exploring the way atoms share information instantly. Water responds to the intent of any vibration it is exposed to; its energy is immediately changed, so its form too changes. We are all linked by water; water is the carrier of life, it is the life blood of the earth; it flows in the veins and arteries of our bodies and in the veins and arteries throughout the earth carrying balance and whatever energy it is imbued with. Dr. Emoto shows that water exposed to the vibrations of love and gratitude, even just the word written on a paper and attached to the bottle, forms a beautiful crystal pattern, and that polluted water can be cleaned by the focus of a prayerful and positive intent.

The function of both Sacred/Circle Dance and water is life giving and life enhancing, and the effect of both is global. They share qualities: they both flow, they change energy, they both balance energies, they are agents of connection; they affect the environment, permeating it with subtle vibrations. The meandering grapevine step which is so common in the Dance is an old Middle Eastern symbol for water; spirals, zig zags and undulating lines, common in Neolithic art, which all feature in the Dance, are ancient symbols for water, the source of life.

Water from springs coming from deep in the earth flows into brooks, into rivers and into the sea; energy from a dancing circle flows out likewise into rivers of light and into the sea of universal consciousness. Every drop of rain increases the water level in the ocean, every dancing circle swells the ocean of positive vibrations on the planet.

12

Challenges

– dealing with difficulties in the circle – the grit in the oyster!

> '*All negativity is caused by an accumulation of psychological time and denial of the present. Unease, anxiety, tension, stress, worry – all forms of fear - are caused by too much future, and not enough presence. Guilt, regret, resentment, grievances, sadness, bitterness and all forms of non forgiveness are caused by too much past, and not enough presence.*'
>
> Eckhart Tolle

Problems occur in a circle as they do everywhere else. Depending on how they are handled they can be disruptive or they can be grand learning experiences.

In the early days of the Dance there was an enthusiastic dancer in Britain who became a teacher almost overnight. Unfortunately he managed to upset almost everyone very quickly! His energy was rampantly 'male' and he brought a dominant and often disharmonious element into the gatherings of the late 1980s. Many people were angry at the displays of ego that felt so counter to the whole spirit of the Dance and wanted him banned. The feeling was that this sort of behaviour and attitude was not appropriate in Sacred/Circle Dance, and some were extremely worried that unless he was stopped the network and the Dance would suffer.

Remember that we were all novices in this, feeling our way, and feeling the awesome responsibility of having been entrusted with this tremendous gift to nurture and promote; we were aware too that this gift was for the healing of the people and not for the greater glory of ourselves. But how were we to act when faced with energy in our midst that felt so at odds with the spirit of what was being promoted, an energy that undoubtedly would put people right off. But 'banning'? That was not only drastic but also seemed to be contrary to the essence of Sacred/Circle Dance, which was for everyone to enjoy, and this guy was a part of 'everyone'!

I felt strongly that banning was not the answer and would set a dangerous precedent. My inner voice was insistent in this instance and in the many similar ones later – *'Let it be! It will be taken care of. Leave it to the angels of the Dance.'* In such a situation I felt it would not work to challenge on the level of the 'problem'; that would only exacerbate the situation and create more bad feeling. I knew there was a constant over-lighting presence of the Dance, a 'Great Circle' up there. I knew it because I not only felt it but saw it regularly, and I also knew that this Sacred/Circle Dance was too important to be 'allowed' to be trashed by the odd ego banging about. *'Let it be'* is still how I feel. In my experience it never works to engage on the level the attack is coming from. If it's 'offered up', it usually sorts itself out. And indeed this dancer found very soon that no one much wanted to come to his group so it fizzled and so did he as a teacher. I have no idea if he continued to dance or what became of him, as he disappeared from the network.

'Anti' elements tend either to become supportive eventually, or they move away from the area, or they get caught up in Line Dancing or Salsa or whatever – that is if they're left to get on with it. However, it is the Dance teacher's job to make the alignment, hold the energy for the group and hold a gateway for the Dance energy to come through and create change. If this is seriously challenged, if it ever comes down to a choice between the needs or neediness of one dancer and the healing work of the group it may be necessary to act. It's one thing to be willing to allow whatever to happen, to go with the flow, but willing has also another meaning – the use of the will. It's a question of looking deeply for the truth of the situation and what the motive of the disruptor is, being absolutely clear and pure in intent oneself and weighing it all up. What a gift they are though, these challengers! They are the best 'life' teachers and initiators and they focus attention on any inner disharmony.

When it comes down to it, the Dance is only as effective as the teachers and dancers are. As we have noted earlier musicians have their instruments, artists their paints and canvases, poets have words, and all we have is ourselves. Our bodies are our instruments and our brush; our canvas is the world. If we want to play a Stradivarius worthily we need dedication, learning and a well cared for instrument, tuned regularly. For the creative genius of the Dance to come through us with maximum effect the 'channel' needs to be clear.

Not long after I began my first group, which had started majestically with twelve dancers, I felt inspired to move from the village into Stroud and booked a hall in the heart of the town. A small circle appeared then gradually numbers dwindled and before long we were down to four, even three, including me. When only a single dancer turned up one evening I was disappointed but undaunted and we danced together; it was a lovely time. The following week she didn't appear nor did anyone else. I waited for 10 minutes and then did the atunement and danced the whole evening through alone with a dedication at then end. The energy in that room throughout the evening was very special, full of light, and far from feeling alone, I felt the hall was full of dancers and at the end energy poured out into the town. From that evening on, people began coming, more and more people came to dance. I had danced my commitment.

When we are ready to 'be wholeheartedly out there' with the Dance, teaching and healing with it, there will be an initiation of some sort to go through, and as soon as we are ready for this (often not on the conscious level, and often resisted!) there will be a test. Are we really committed to this, what price are we prepared to pay to bring this energy to the earth, and to speak our truth about it? Are we prepared to have our ego edges rubbed smooth, and personal agendas released so we can be clearer channels of the Dance Light in its full purity and power? Can we let not only criticism but also adulation pass through us, and see that the ones who adulate are in fact seeing something that is dormant in **them**. They may see a free spirit and a fulfilment of commitment, which is exactly what they aspire to. Can we let them see past us to what lies behind – to the Dance and to their own spirits? These initiations happen to challenge our commitment and to show us where the edges and agendas are, so they too can be offered in service.

If a teacher inadvertently rocks the boat and challenges people's comfort zones and the tactics they come up with to avoid really letting the Dance move through them, up comes trouble! A light shone into a secret dark recess may be far too uncomfortable and if so it may be projected on to the perpetrator! I've learnt over the years that these attacks are never about me/us, they are only about the 'attackers', so if I am able to just accept and see them as just 'another one of me' doing their dance, I have nothing to defend and immediately they stop being 'attackers', the mist clears and I see they are just people showing me their wound.

In 1987 I co-focalised the Harmonic Concordance Dance Camp in Wales for 400 plus dancers. All, or nearly all, were present in the huge main lodge for the first 'pow-wow'. I introduced the gathering and suggested each spoke or not as they felt. I said something about keeping our sharing brief as we were so many and then we would be able to share communion in the Dance and something to the effect that the deepest and truest sharing happens in silence. The talking stick was in the centre for anyone to take as they felt like it and one after another – it felt like everyone and forever to me – the stick was taken and turned on me. How dare I suggest the sharing be short, they had every right to talk as long as they wished! Attack followed attack: some were spittingly aggressive and I felt them as not just an attack on what I'd said but on me! There was some positive sharing too of course – funny how they slip out of memory.

Throughout the pow-wow which lasted almost three hours I had to sit still, my calm exterior masking the turmoil and pain inside, and deal with the feelings; riding the horror; longing for the ground to open up and swallow me; struggling to keep hold of some tiny life belt of truth and centre.

At the lowest point, when I felt *'I'm going to lose it!'*, a dancing soul sister took the stick and for – how long? – five, ten minutes, a lifetime? she danced. She simply, and in silence, danced! Like a panther she circled around and around facing each and everyone, dancing the aggression and the fear and the pain, dancing the oneness, and coming back and back again to dance in front of me bringing me the strength of the angels, honouring, supporting, affirming and above all loving me. She danced it all! The energy in that circle when she finished was Silent Light. Even so there were a few die-hard jackals that had smelt blood, but now I could feel the angel's wings around me, now I could see it through!

People feel safe dancing and being part of a circle, as they do with all experiences which have become familiar and non-threatening, but eventually complacency can creep in. A dancing circle can become a very powerful Comfort Zone, but Comfort Zones can inhibit growth.

Sometimes when people first discover the Dance they may feel challenged, but after a while, as it all becomes familiar and confidence grows, they relax and feel safe from challenges, or rather feel assured that any challenges will be within the context of this haven and therefore non-threatening. They reach a plateau and settle down on it. Changing the analogy, when something rocks the boat, shaking complacency and presenting a challenge to grow and expand, fear in the form of defence (and it can sometimes be quite aggressive defence) may erupt in order to protect the safe parameter. After a while, the sense of quest and the urge to use the Dance to get higher or deeper or further can atrophy.

It is of course possible to confine yourself to being a 'beginner' for ever more, to take the dances at face value and simply have fun and deny yourself the thrill of discovering and expanding. The issue is – what is this Dance really about? Is it about growing and opening up to the whole Self, is it about risking the empty ocean, or is it about taking a short trip, finding a safe harbour, and settling for that? It **can** be a way of initiation, an ongoing process of dancing into complete Self-hood, but it's also perfectly possible for it to be just another form of physical exercise, another form of dance that allows the dancers to remain within their safe boundaries!

To go deeply into Sacred/Circle Dance means that when a safe boundary has become a wall blocking growth it can be gracefully challenged and released or expanded; in other words, as the sense of the Self develops through the power of the Dance, the structure holding it becomes too small and can dissolve through the energy of the dancing; the dancer then moves into a new freedom until the next time they don't fit inside their 'house' and have to extend the walls again. It can be an ongoing process if so they intend – build, demolish, extend; build, demolish, extend, until finally no walls are needed and the 'house' is the limitless universe – or 'home'!

What is to be done though with a deliberately disruptive element? With a dancer, for instance, that needs and takes so much attention that the circle loses cohesion? Easier first to say what **doesn't** work. What doesn't work is to give attention or to engage on the same level. It's not the place for attention, and engaging on the level the disruption is on will fragment the circle and lose the Dance energy. What is needed is intense focus. The more deeply centred the teacher becomes the more the circle will hold and the quicker the disruption will lose power.

Energy follows thought so concentrating on the bigger picture, on the glue of the Cosmic Circle above to hold the circle together, and even sending a thought to the 'guardian angel' of the disruptive dancer requesting assistance can work wonders!

The energy of the circle draws this energy to it, rather as moths are attracted to light. The vortex of light created by the circle pulls this negating energy into it and transforms it. This negating energy can be fed by thought and attitude until it becomes so strong it can operate by itself, and so destructive entities and individual thought forms are free to move around looking for somebody or occasionally an animal with a similar vibration energy through which it can work. In most cases the 'host' is unconscious of what is operating through them.

I have said that the vortex of light created by the circle transforms these energies and there has never been an occasion in my experience when this hasn't happened; however, depending on the size and power of the negating energy and depending too on the proportion of dancers there are with clear, light energy, there may be what amounts to a battle between the light or love and its opposition, sometimes bringing intense pain until it is cleared. We will look further at this energy in the chapter on the changes brought about through the Dance.

Very occasionally the 'host' is fully conscious and calls on and uses 'negative' power for its own ends. This is not fun! These powers are real and dangerous if channelled and directed knowingly. I learnt this the hard way! I had known this charismatic Swedish man for a number of years; he danced in my Danceshops in Sweden, he meditated, and was known as a dedicated light worker. A change happened in him, however: he became a 'Teacher', almost a guru, with the requisite crowd of adoring female followers. One summer I was feeling really uncomfortable around him but I was also intrigued enough by his sugges- tion to meet him for a picnic out in nature that I agreed, even though I felt we had little to say to each other. It was pleasant enough but when he dropped me off in the village he was barely managing to be civil and roared off almost before my feet were on the ground.

I thought no more of it at the time but the next evening, the Dance evening I was leading in the community (to my surprise Mr. Charisma didn't show!), developed into one of the worst experiences of my life. I 'lost the plot' of the evening, found it hard to say coherent sentences even speak, my vision was blurred, and I had difficulty remembering the simplest dances that I knew as well as my own name. It got steadily worse; a pain started in my head that became so intense I felt I'd go mad, I was nauseous and finally could hardly move any part of my body.

Somehow the dancing happened and with only my two closest friends realising how serious things were. The evening ended and I collapsed with a dangerously high temperature, pain beyond belief, and a huge festering lump on my lip. I was rescued and cared for with great love and by the next evening was recovering enough to review what had happened and seek some understanding.

I saw that the charismatic gentleman had wanted what I had, wanted my energy, my power, and that his intent for our sunny picnic was to steal it. Clearly though it had not been available and this was his revenge. A painful lesson in understanding how destructive energy can work.

There may be occasions, however, with these energies in a circle when even the focus and centring doesn't work! It has happened only once to me, a never-to-be-forgotten nightmare, but this is taking us into darker waters.

From the first moments of that Dance Gathering many years ago, there was something strange going on. People I knew well were acting completely out of character; anger erupted from a docile woman over a trivial incident with a cup of tea in the kitchen, something that normally would have been ignored or become a source of amusement. There were forty of us gathered for the weekend, and on the Saturday evening I was to lead a ceremony (a less loaded word I feel than ritual). Part of this ceremony was to be a spiral dance in which we were to dance in to the centre, turn there, and dance out again, without holding hands. It was carefully explained and basically simple, especially as all were experienced dancers and most were teachers.

There was a heavy atmosphere around before we started. I recognised the presence of life-destroying vibes from the difficulty I was having speaking and forming simple sentences. I had been feeling uncomfortable around one particular woman all weekend, and was not the only one who had had difficulties with her energy in circles in the past. It seemed significant when I realised later that she and her three close friends were all dressed in unrelieved black.

The dance starts beautifully, bodies coming closer and closer together as the spiral begins to tighten towards the centre. Suddenly there is a disturbance ahead and to my horror I realise that the 'particular woman' has broken line and is leading people back out although they haven't yet reached the centre. I haven't, and **I'm** leading the line, so there is no way they could have! Confusion spreads like wild fire, the form of the spiral is lost, and this woman is dancing towards me with an expression on her face that is spine chilling. From the look she gives me it is clear that what she is doing is intentional. She has deliberately sabotaged the ceremony. The thing was ruined! It wasn't a film, I couldn't shout out '*OK cut!*' I couldn't speak of what I had witnessed in that look.

What to do in such a situation? I kept dancing mechanically while reviewing options frantically. There weren't any! Then from somewhere came the prayer – '*Give me courage to change the things I can change, humility to accept the things I can't and wisdom to know the difference*'. I did the only thing I could do – re-gained focus, and holding the spiral pattern firmly continued to dance it and somehow moved through the chaotic mess and completed the spiral; miraculously we did all eventually come out into a circle once more.

Bizarre and unpleasant things continued happening the next day. Four of us escaped and found our way into a wood where we sat on the ground leaning against a huge tree holding hands and seeking an explanation.

Before telling of the realisation that came to us I will reiterate the statement I made at the beginning of this book, that all interpretations and meanings contained here are my own personal opinions.

We had the strong feeling that what was happening was a karmic replay of an event way in the past – centuries in the past – and as we opened to that possibility images flooded in of a temple of dance in Ancient Greece at the time of a take-over, a time when the original worship of a 'goddess' was being overthrown by priests and a male god. At once light dawned and we understood the polarisation that had been happening in our 20th century circle. Incidents that were inexplicable and disturbing now made sense.

Maybe, as it seemed, we had come together again as a group in the 20th century to re-live this and work it through: to hold the integrity of the 'temple', and the sacredness of the Dance this time. The realisation helped us to hold centre and stay clear in this intent for the rest of the event. There have been other instances of karmic healing through the Dance over the years, though none so dramatic!

Maybe Sacred/Circle Dancers are part of a 'group soul'; people who somehow share a common spiritual origin, or maybe who all signed the same 'contract' before coming to earth and have incarnated together again in order to bring the gift of Dance to the earth at this crucial changeover time, and maybe to finish what we have often started in the past. Who knows? It would certainly help to explain the ease and familiarity dancers often instantly feel with each other, that sense of knowing people you've never met before the moment you clap eyes on them.

13

Focus on the Centre?
– the significance of the centre of the circle

'To circle around the centre is to be in constant relationship with the
Source of Being.'

Unknown

The centre of the circle symbolises the inner centre of the body, the still
point inside where all the strands of the web of our lives and of our being
meet and fuse in our divine oneness. We experience, when dancing
around a centre 'altar' (and this is a major reason for marking the
centre physically), that when we are connected to our own inner centre
we automatically become one with all and directly experience ourselves
as part of the Centre of Life, the Source, the All That Is, the Oneness. We
know ourselves to be the centre of the universe even as we dance on the
periphery of the circle. We are in the same step the 'i' and the 'I'.

There are many dances where the focus is the other people in the
circle. **Enas Mythos**, the Greetings Dance from the Greek island of
Kos, is the classic example of this; in the early days it began every
session and was consequently the very first dance people learnt. As it is
a greetings dance the idea is to greet everyone in the circle before the
end. Even during this particular dance, however, it may at times be
helpful to focus on the centre too, as a way of greeting the inner self
and being totally present at the start of a session.

Different dances call for different focuses. If I'm dancing a meditation
dance I won't be looking around the circle seeking eye contact with other
dancers. Some dances are inward with the outer gaze unfocused; some
have the focus on the earth, some on the centre, some up above.

A well-known way to calm the mind and come into a meditative
state is to focus the attention on a candle flame; the 'altar' at the centre
of the circle can have this effect, it echoes the centre within the bodies

84

of the dancers and helps to bring the dancers in, not only to themselves, but also into the collective place at the source where all are one. A centre-piece also serves the practical purpose of marking centre so that the perimeter can gauge its alignment; in other words it helps to stop the circle wandering about the room!

I often use a round tray on a silk scarf of varying hue. Most of these scarves are riddled with tiny holes as if the silk worms are now busy devouring what they once created; this is one of the built-in hazards of this work as one of the things I like to have in the centre is a stick of incense which manages on a fairly regular basis to drop minute quantities of ash on to the silk scarf rather than on the tray or the floor. I have many such pockmarked scarves. I also have a voluptuous female clay figure seated in naked splendour in a cross-legged position on the tray and holding a nightlight[10] in her lap.

Usually I will have a representation of earth, air, fire and water – a crystal, a feather, a candle and a shell for example. I enjoy making a garden in the centre with a tray of earth, rocks – maybe moss covered – tiny shells and flowers! Always flowers! The centre invariably represents what is happening in nature at that time of year; spring will see snow-drops, buds and a fresh green; summer – flowers, flowers, flowers, feathers and bright, rich colours; autumn – ripened corn/grain, fruit, leaves turning gold, yellow and brown; and winter – bare earth, twigs, crystals, rocks, dried flowers, maybe a tiny cave built of moss-covered rocks holding a nightlight.

In this way the connection with the natural rhythms and our roots in the earth is maintained. When we dance in these circles nature dances with us; the nature beings – the flower fairies, the elves, gnomes, dryads, and undines are part of our circle celebrating the earth and our return to the 'garden'.

A few years ago I was drawn to make an appointment with a well-known Canadian clairvoyant in British Columbia. She is booked up far ahead so I regarded it as serendipity that there just 'happened' to be a free appointment during the short time I was in Victoria. Everything she gave me has been and continues to be of immense help. She 'saw' me dancing (without knowing what I do), and got very excited about it. *Fairies surround you,* she said or words to this effect. *You need to call your dancing Fairy Dance or something of the sort, and – always! – you must have flowers around you – they are **very** important for you,* so flowers dance with us in the centre.

Candles, which I always light at the centre, symbolise the fire of the sun, the fire in the centre of the earth, the fire in the heart and the belly, the light at the centre of each of the dancers and the fire of the spirit. In the

A centre 'altar'. Photo by Esbjorn Aneer.

Celtic tradition the hearth is where the veil between worlds is thin, so here there can be communication with other dimensions. In the Native American tradition, the smoke from the fire represents the prayers to Great Spirit and in the Sweat Lodge the fire at the centre is for purification. In Mongolia it is believed that the fire is the centre of the universe; in their homes the fire is always at the centre as in most other earth based nature societies, be it in a tipi or a yurt or a mud hut, and this is considered to be the most sacred place of the dwelling. A circle with a dot in the centre is the astronomical symbol for the sun. So the candle at the centre of the circle is earth fire, sun fire, body fire, the fire of spirit and our communion with it; it is cleansing fire; it travels our prayers; it is life-sustaining; and it is the spark of new beginnings.

14

Diversity and 'Variations'
– the individual, the group, the importance of the form

> *'We have become not a melting pot but a beautiful mosaic. Different people, different beliefs, different yearnings, different hopes, different dreams.'*
>
> Jimmy Carter

In tune with the energy of co-creativity and group responsibility that is increasing on the planet as we move further into the spirit of the Aquarian age, the 'body' of Sacred/Circle Dance maintains its health through a very loose network. There are currently 750 listed committed dancers and teachers, and countless groups and events apart from this network. There are no rules, no bosses or any suggestion of a hierarchy, simply many circles, many teachers and many approaches. We are all individuals and one of the greatest gifts of this dancing network is that there **is** no regimentation, no standardisation, no one accepted way of 'doing' the Dance.

There is beauty and unity and power in our diversity simply because of this freedom, simply **because** there are no rules, **because** each expresses the truth that is theirs and the unique facet of the Dance that resonates with that. All the expressions of Sacred/Circle Dance are equally valid and each is an important cell in the body of the whole. Everyone finds their own way and their own level and truth in the Dance and one of the triumphs of such a long-standing and widely scattered community is that this freedom of diversity within unity has been maintained.

There is diversity in the way the Dance is presented; each circle will inevitably be unique, as it will reflect the individual focaliser/teacher and the dancers within it. I have come to realise that there are many different types of circles and many different things happening under the umbrella of Circle Dance. I was struck dumb the first time someone came up to me at the end of an evening and said *'Thank you, I never realised this dancing was spiritual'*. How, I wondered, and still wonder, can it **not** be? but for many it clearly is not, yet gives other gifts.

I know of one group that has been dancing together for years who just love talking to each other; even while dancing they chatter, seldom about the dancing but domestic and personal chat; and they always drop hands the second the last note of music fades after each dance. They must get a lot from it, they keep coming. Some circles, maybe this is an example, are about community and become a strong support for each other, helping each other through crises and celebrating birthdays and hearing each other's stories, and this is the main glue and focus of the group. The Dance serves people in so many ways, and all are positive, all are healing.

I have danced in circles where the main focus was the other people in the circle. Indeed in the 1980s there was criticism from Findhorn of the circles south of the border for having a centrepiece in the circle – flowers or a candle or whatever – as they considered the focus to be the people who were there. To me this loses a major dimension of the Dance, as will have been seen in the previous chapter, 'Focus on the Centre?', and maybe this is partly what people mean when they comment on the lack of spiritual meaning in some circles.

I once danced in a circle where there was not one single second of silence between any of the dances the entire evening; no energy was held, not even after the very last, deep dance, even then at such a moment the circle immediately broke into social mode. I left feeling cheated at not having had the opportunity to allow the dances to penetrate every cell or the energy of the evening to integrate fully. Of course I feel the energy during the dance, but I feel the inner essence integrate completely in me during the stillness and silence – that is when deep communication happens.

Each teacher has her or his own style and gift to bring to the Dance; some use their skill at humour as their main teaching 'device' and enable easy learning and confidence through the wonderful relaxing medium of laughter; some employ 'Eros' and their sensuality/sexuality to pass the Dance on, some through enormous vitality and enthusiasm; some through a gentle and quietly centred way which calms minds and anxieties and brings the circle into a receptive and meditative state. There must be as many different types of circles as there are people teaching! One way is not better than another, they are all valid, they all answer a need, and they are all expressions of the one unifying spirit.

If there is no authority telling you how things are to be done, and what's right and what isn't, diversity will flourish. This allows a glorious creative freedom of expression; it can also mean a loss of authenticity, even of integrity.

When I learnt the first dances early in the 1980s, we were given the steps, country of origin, and meaning, if it were known. It was all beautifully simple – this dance, for example, is called **Eno Bushi**, it is a rice-planting and harvesting dance from Japan. Several years on, a new authority announces that this dance is not in fact **Eno Bushi** but **Tanko Bushi**, and is not a rice-planting dance but a coal-mining dance! And so it has gone on – one absolute after another crumbling before wave after wave of new information from new 'authorities'.

It happens with the steps of some of the dances too. Suddenly we are told that the slip step to the centre and the two slow sways we have always found so meaningful should in fact be a grapevine to right and a grapevine to the left! It has been extremely confusing, at times irritating. Who to believe? The new 'authority' speaks with such force and conviction, but the original version came with integrity from a respected teacher! Does it really matter if it's slip steps or walking steps if the feel is right? Well yes it does and no it doesn't!

Faced with this dilemma so many times, I decided finally to make up my own mind and dance it the way that felt right to me. Unless the new version really feels more authentic or adds something of value, I stay with what I first learnt. The movements in the Japanese dance work equally well for planting rice or digging coal; I prefer the way I learnt it first as rice but usually say that it is also thought to be a coal-mining dance. Sometimes I feel the 'new' version works better, sometimes a bit of one and a slice of the other! It is a living tradition after all, not a museum collection, and provided the foundation place is integrity and commitment to the spirit of the Dance there is room for all versions.

The folkdance societies have given and still do give a vital service in maintaining authenticity in the traditional dances, keeping them as pure as possible. I feel we owe it to the tradition, to the people who danced and still dance these dances as a crucial and integral part of their lives, and to the cultures they spring from, to honour with as much accuracy as we can this great heritage.

Also as good craftspeople it is important we keep all the dances as pure as possible; wherever they come from; if the steps are allowed to get sloppy, they will, like any tools that are allowed to rust or get blunt, lose their ability to perform effectively.

Kalamatianos. Sketch by Bernhard Wosien by kind permission of Maria-Gabriele Wosien.

Having said that, a rigid attachment to 'How It Is' and 'The Right Way' to dance a dance limits the possibility to evolve and the free movement of creative spirit. I have often wondered, when one 'authentic version' meets and clashes forcibly with another 'authentic version', how do we **know**? **Both** may be authentic!

Nowadays dances are being choreographed by one or occasionally by two people and everyone knows the origin of these dances and authenticity can be checked – surely back in time the old dances would have evolved out of the local community. Villages were isolated from each other so when a shared aspect of their life needed to be expressed in dance each community would express it in its own way. All are valid. It doesn't work to come at such things with a sophisticated analytical northern European mind.

It's a different matter with the countless new dances pouring out of the creative springs of so many dancers now. There is only one 'authentic' version of the dance because the choreographer is known. It's easy to check when a different version of a modern dance is taught, the authority is the choreographer. Variations do happen, it's referred to as 'Chinese Whispers' where messages passed on person to person get altered; it's bound to happen, it goes with being human.

I confess I only dance in other teachers' circles if I know and fully respect their integrity. I have had too many uncomfortable experiences in the past of well-loved dances being taught differently from how I learnt and have always danced them.

Sometimes the changes are slight and I can still keep the energy of the dance but when it's a 'classic' dance, for instance, if it's the Greek national dance **Kalamatianos** that is being taught wrongly, seriously wrongly as I once experienced it, my tolerance fades! With a dance such as that I can't say 'it's a different version'. No! It's not an acceptable variation (and there are many versions of this dance), it's just 'wrong'! My body can't and won't dance it that way. It's a horrible experience because I don't want to speak up and put the teacher on the line but neither can I stay and do something that just feels so alien. I have very occasionally had to leave the circle at such instances.

There have also been times when I have been taught a very different version of a dance which I myself have choreographed! Then I have, tactfully, drawn attention to it, all the time wishing the floor would open up and swallow me.

On one memorable occasion, however, the teacher, along with a couple of the other dancers who joined in support, actually argued with me about the steps! *'No we do it like this.'* They stuck to their 'Chinese' version, and I had a painful time trying to dance it, all the time vowing never to join an unknown circle again. Such absolute 'right-ness' is far from the spirit of Sacred/Circle Dance. The only absolutes here are the truth of the Dance and respect for each other.

15

Quality versus Quantity
– going deeper versus acquiring more and more new dances!

'What, at this moment, is lacking?'

Zen Master Rinzai

I started my first Dance group in 1983 with 12 dancers and 12 dances! It was enough of both! Now I have upwards of 800 dances filed away. I say 'away' because it's impossible to keep that number of dances on the boil or even simmering. Many have not been aired for several years and don't resonate at the present time: maybe they will rebirth themselves at a later date; some were immensely important for a while and then their time ran out, maybe they had done what they came to do, and now they sit around adding numbers to a database. Perhaps their time too will come again, and that specific energy will again be meaningful and useful.

I find the only way to handle such a huge number of dances is to select a smaller pool from this vast ocean and work from that for a while. Dances added to the ocean recently will be in this pool and always my choice for this dance pool is influenced by the season; certain dances relate to certain times and festivals. For example, one dance may have a distinct summer flavour, another may encapsulate the energy of the winter solstice, another Imbolc or Candlemas, the beginning of the Celtic spring. Some are created specifically for a particular time, like **Litha** (the old Anglo-Saxon name for Midsummer), and would feel inappropriate danced in November, as would **Descent** danced at the spring equinox!

Life was simpler in the days when I could somehow hold all the dances I knew in my awareness at once, and often I long to have that simplicity again. So many wonderful dances get neglected for long periods of time; they simply have to cease to exist for me. There is a tremendous hunger for new dances among both many teachers and dancers and I wonder why this is. Maybe it's a sign of the times, of the restless seeking for new possessions and experiences gripping the mainstream of the privileged western world that is rubbing off on the network. Sad, though, if it means the old dances are forgotten. Maybe it's the search for ways to express what is evolving and not yet charted in any way.

This hunger means that sometimes people attempt to learn new dances from the notation in Dance booklets. Each dance has its own particular energy as does each person on earth. Would I know you simply from reading your CV or hearing your voice on the phone, or would I know you through your eyes and the energy of your presence? The dances are alive; and learning dances from written notes rather than directly from another person loses so much of their living, magical energy. The steps **can** be learnt that way but the **essence** of the Dance is subtle and beyond the steps; it is transmitted body to body, spirit to spirit; a sacred trust from the Great Circle, from the origins of time.

The Dance is a healthy being; it is a living tradition that is constantly creating new forms and expanding boundaries; expressing the aspirations and feelings that are unique to these times, as well as those that are eternal and universal. The greatest benefit is in taking the gifts and jewels of the past and adding to them what of quality is specific to now. Maybe it's a sign of the superficiality of the time we live in; rushing from one experience to the next leaves no time or opportunity to explore what lies beneath, to live deeply, and quality is sacrificed for quantity.

The more the old dances are danced the more treasures of insights and understanding and transforming energy they yield. They richly reward in-depth exploration, but it's a question of choice; you can go as deeply as you desire with the Dance – as with most experiences – or you can stay on the surface when what you get will be a surface experience.

To illustrate the richness inside the dances just waiting to be explored we can look at Enas Mythos, the Greek greetings dance mentioned in the previous chapter. (Bernhard Wosien introduced this dance at Findhorn as a dance from the time of the Knights Templar, but left it unclear whether he had adapted the traditional dance that he learned on the island of Kos.)

The dance starts with the left foot moving into the circle; the dancer moves forward intuitively in greeting; it is not thought out – rather the movement is instinctive, like a child, open and delighted with life, coming towards you. Then it is the conscious rational self – who has learnt the importance of recognising and honouring boundaries – who makes a move away, taking a step back with the right foot; and it is the same rational thinking self who decides when it is time to move on in life to the next meeting, to the next phase, stepping to the side on the right foot.

Each stage of the dance makes a deliberate statement; each is a separate conscious act, marked by bringing both feet together after each move. So – I greet you (stepping towards centre) and spend time with you (feet closing together), I give you space (stepping back) and come again into my own centre and into the moment (feet together), before I then move on (stepping sideways) and adjust to that by being present in myself (feet together).

The little knee bends on each close step symbolise the undulating sea, the sea which surrounds the island of Kos whence comes this dance. The sea is so important in Greek life, the sea that folds me in the embrace of Neptune when I leave the harbour; the sea that takes me away on my journey and brings me back home once more.

The arms are crossed in front of the body, right over left on the forearm; the looping up the right arm, over the head and down the left arm links the dancers strongly together. This is symbolic of the universal chain of life; the pattern formed by the energy recalls the shape of the Egyptian ankh – the symbol of life. The energy travels up

Egyptian ankh.

from the earth, through both the hands and up both arms, over the head and down the opposite arm to pass to the next dancer.

Physical life is symbolised by the cross and eternal life by the circle. The ankh was believed to give life as well as sustain it. The circle or loop represents the womb or yoni of the feminine, while the vertical pole is the masculine phallus, so both energies are united here, thus creating new life. The pole is in fact in two layers which supports the picture of the double energy stream coming up from the earth. The ankh is also clearly a representation of the human being (with the loop the head, the pole the body and the cross the arms) who when she/he brings the polarity energies into harmony in the body lives eternal life while in a physical body.

The arms form the cross of St. Andrew, the diagonal cross, so the dancer's body creates an eight pointed star as it moves – the firm vertical axis which is emphasised by the knee bends up and down, the horizontal plane on the side step and the diagonal cross of the arms.

This is the dance that traditionally opens a Dance session. As we have seen it is said to be a greeting dance that was danced by or with the Knights Templar on their return home from their exploits and adventures. Whether or not this is apocryphal it is a great way to greet the other dancers in the circle. Frequently now in circles in Britain it is danced with a V hold. The practical reason for this is that it is natural for the dancers to make the step back out of the circle bigger than the step towards the centre; it can be quite threatening to be in such an intimate hold and then to be expected to move even closer to people you may never have seen before! *Phew, a step back, let's take space here!* However, this soon produces a 'strangle hold' as the arms straighten and get pulled further and further out of their sockets; it's extremely uncomfortable and probably not the best introduction to the Dance!

We have a wonderful example in this dance of 'doing and being'! Taking it as the dance of the returning Knights Templars, we have the three sections of their journeying – the going away from, the moving on and the returning home. After each move, bringing the feet together and bending the knees allows the dancers to **be** where they are. There is a beautiful feeling of sinking gratefully into the earth and enjoying the 'being', after the 'doing' of the travelling step. Interesting to note that for this part two beats are allowed, while for the travelling 'doing' there is only one, so the dancer learns that 'being' is more valuable than 'doing'. Interesting too that there are nine steps – one for each of the original nine Templar Knights?

When a dance is referred to as 'advanced' it usually means intricate footwork, many sections and/or fast movement. What is considered an

95

easy dance is slow with very few simple steps. However, I wonder whether you find it easier to walk briskly or very, very slowly. Certainly it's easier to cycle at a good pace than to go at the wobbly snail's speed of those slow cycle 'races' we set up as kids. There is a discipline and a focus needed in a slow dance, a superabundance of presence.

Laura Shannon writing in the Winter 2004 edition of Grapevine writes that Yiorgos Lazaron of the Dora Stratou Theatre says that a slow dance is more difficult than a fast one. '*The fewer and simpler the steps*', Laura goes on, '*the more advanced the dance, because of the inner energy that is activated undistracted by high speeds and intricate step sequences, we must focus fully on the inner work required in order to get what the dance has to offer, as well as to give what the dance demands*'.

I recall walking sessions at Drama School when we would attempt to emulate the movement implicit in Greek statues and frescoes where the garments swoop and swirl round the goddess' body as she walks; it is as if you can see the currents of air she is creating by her movement. It was a painstaking exercise; performed as slowly as possible as if at the interface between movement and stillness; each step was a detailed choreography in itself, balance, flow and grace being the keynotes. Very like the Buddhist Walking Meditation where you match step to breath and where every individual step entails a whole sequence of movements. Ven. Pannyavaro teaching Insight Meditation says – '*For the first five minutes you can note just three parts of the step: 'lifting', 'pushing', 'dropping'. Then mentally note or label each step part by part building up the noting to its six component parts: 'raising', 'lifting', 'pushing', 'dropping', 'touching' and 'pressing' – concurrent with the actual experience of the movement.*' Well, if you remember it took us a quite a while – 12 months on average – just to learn to stand and to move one foot in front of the other!

In Enas Mythos while there isn't this kind of deliberation in the steps an awareness and a discipline is required to dance it 'perfectly'. It's not so vital with a V hold but in the crossed arm hold it is essential to match the length of step forward to the step backward (checking your inner ease with this – *do I tend to pull back or push forward in life* etc). There must also be awareness of the arms that they don't slide up but stay loosely crossed on the forearm. It's also necessary to gauge the side step to be just the right distance to the right to keep your place exact in the circle and to avoid scrunching your neighbour's toes!

Of course this is not thrown at the circle when the dance is first taught but it illustrates the difference an awareness of style makes. Enas Mythos with a V hold is a beautiful dance but a dimension is lost.

Bob Minney playing for the Dance in Dorset. Photo by Brendan Buesnel.

No dance is the same experience twice so there is no possibility of boredom. The chemistry will be different with each circle, the time of day or night affects how the dance will come alive, and the particular focus of the session if there is one. Repeating a dance takes you deeper; three times seems to be the magic number, something happens with the third repetition, a deeper grounding that brings the depth of the dance into the body. What takes the dancer even deeper is to dance a dance for a much longer time then the average five minutes, half an hour up to and even over an hour. I had a superb experience of 'Quality' long dancing with only a handful of dances for five days to live music with a man who both composes and plays for the Dance. Bob Minney is an inspiring musician, and as dance and music, dancers and musician, merged into one the dances opened up new dimensions of themselves and took us all on a journey round the universe and into a deeper dimension of **our**selves!

Whereas for an evening of Dance a wide spectrum of dances works best, giving a satisfying variety of energies which taken together are healing, I could run an entire Danceshop on, for example, a dance like the **Omal Garassari**.[11]

The form of **Omal Garassari** is simple, yet it contains everything – focus, balance of energies, grounded lightness, being present, gentle power, and a style that shakes everything up, clears out old stuck energy and realigns the body. It teaches the importance of having a strong structure and of being flexible around it; it teaches how to be centred in your truth whichever way you turn, and whatever you see. It teaches commitment, discipline, and focus.

To honour this dance and glean its gifts, however, those three qualities are needed: there has to be a 'commitment' – to stay present in the body; 'focus' – to handle the changes of direction; and 'discipline' – to maintain the precision of the small steps and the alignment of the entire body. Think of a spinning top, it is movement and stillness combined. The movement can only happen because of its centre pole being still and aligned vertically. The steps of **Omal Garassari** are strong, the skeleton – the centre pole – firm and upright, and around this vertical structure the cells of the body vibrate – the spinning – so the body learns to be free within structure. Quite enough for a weekend Danceshop!

16

Living in the Body
– effect of the Dance on body parts and energy flow

> *'To really **be** in the body*
> *is to feel the body from within,*
> *to feel the life **inside** the body*
> *and thereby come to know*
> *that you are beyond*
> *the outer form.*
> *So it is with*
> *the inner energy of the Dance*
> *and the outer form of the steps'*
>
> Unknown

A dance such as **Omal Garassari** when danced often enough brings the dancer's consciousness into the body and an awareness of what the body is doing. It becomes a moving meditation. For most people this awareness happens only in the very rudimentary ways of moving them from *a* to *b* and getting things done. These are mechanical actions; a simple message from the brain and motor nerves automatically respond while the consciousness may well be elsewhere.

Even among dancers there is sometimes a surprising lack of aware-ness of their bodies. There's the well-known right/left foot confusion; one reason this happens is that the opposite side of the circle from the teacher has a mirror image of what she or he is doing, which can take some time to adjust to. I point out the anklet I wear as a marker to signify my left foot. Often heard in circles, especially when there are dancers who are new, is the phrase – *'Oh! The **other** left!'*; and any embarrassment is dispelled in the laughter.

An instruction like *'raise the arms in front to heart height'* can produce a forest of waving branches, some even reaching for the stars. The instruction may be repeated many times, and for a while arms do indeed all rise to the horizontal and no higher, but within a few moments the forest returns. It takes time, it takes patience, and it takes commitment, to really inhabit and know the body and take full responsibility for it and what it does.

In Britain we are still suffering from the effects of the Victorian era, the Christian denial of the body, and the overemphasis on the intellect in education. There is now an upsurge of interest in self healing, in exploring the causes and effects of illness and taking responsibility for personal health, and what is also needed is a dance form such as Sacred/Circle Dance which brings the spirit in to live in the healing body temple, and which teaches not only awareness of the body moving in space and time and many different ways of extending and refining this knowledge but also teaches movements which are healing and empowering.

Feet

Through the feet we keep a strong physical connection with the earth. We ground the energy of the Dance through the feet and give it to the earth. This becomes especially powerful when dancing barefoot outside on the earth. The sole of the foot also contains a map of the body, so dancing in a sacred manner affects the entire body through this magical connection with the Earth Mother. She feeds the body and the spirit directly through the soles of our feet when we dance on her with awareness. Both the earth and the dancer receive a healing and invigorating massage.

Hips

The pelvis is the gateway to life and ancient people believed this was true not only in the sense of physical birth but also in the sense of birthing our own life energy. It is where in Taoist tradition the Tan Tien resides, seen as a radiating ball of light; in the Tantric tradition it houses the Kundalini, the powerful energy that is coiled at the base of the spine waiting to be guided up through the body to bring enlightenment; in matriarchal traditions it is the home of the Goddess; and it is also where the primary energies reside – basic survival, sexuality and self esteem – that relate to grounded physicality and that are the foundation of ourselves in our bodies.

Dances from the Gypsy or Rom tradition use the hips freely. There can be hip lifts, circles, lemniscates, shimmies, all activating this area of power, freeing up shame or guilt from past conditioning concerning sexuality, and massaging the self esteem. What is now called Egyptian Dance, and more commonly Belly Dancing (the word may come from an Egyptian rhythm 'baladi'), comes from the ancient Greek temples to Aphrodite, the goddess of love, beauty and sexuality and are dances of women's spirituality. The teachers in these temples understood the connection of this area of the body with the spirit, and the dances, far from being danced to 'turn men on', were sacred dances where women explored, celebrated and built their sexual/spiritual power.

Knees

The knees can hold trapped 'negative' energy, particularly in the psyches of women. Knees bend in servitude to a god, a lord or a husband. Kneeling implies inferiority, humility, and devotion to something considered higher than oneself. Pilgrims during the Crusades were obliged to make their symbolic journey to the Holy Land through the labyrinths on the floor of medieval cathedrals on their knees. Knees held rigid and legs marching straight signify dominance, superiority, military power and a crushing of opposition.

Major meridians from the main organs of the body run through the legs – energy lines from the liver, kidneys, stomach and spleen. In Chinese tradition the 'negative' emotion stored in the liver is anger; in the kidneys, fear; and in the stomach, the inability to accept or digest what life brings up. Walking or dancing with rigid knees can damage the nerves of the spine and sends an unloving message to the body. It is important to keep the knees loose while dancing and in many dances flexed knees are a vital part of the style; they bob up and down on each off beat between the steps. This is an exhilarating movement and frees up locked energies from these organs, which can then travel down the legs into the earth – the great recycler of our energy!

17

Birthing Dances
– my experiences as a choreographer

'Your children are not your children. They are the sons and daughters of life's longing for itself. They come through you but not from you.'

'The Prophet'
Kilhal Gibran

Sacred/Circle Dance is a living tradition, growing and moving with the times. Unlike folk dance (with the exception of Israeli folk dance) it includes newly choreographed dances. The collection of dances that Bernhard Wosien originally took to Findhorn included some of his own choreographies, although the percentage of new dances was small, approximately one quarter to three quarters traditional dances. We are living at a pivotal point in the human story and while there are universal themes that are applicable to all people at all stages of evolution, there are specific issues and energies of the present time to be recognised and expressed. Dances are constantly being created from the experiences and needs and yearnings of Now, and the music of Now carries them. So the circles dance to pop, reggae, synthesised, meditative and classical music in addition to the ethnic folk music.

I am reluctant to speak of choreographing the dances attributed to me, it feels rather that they **come to** me. The first arrived sometime in 1984/5, there are now over 60. These dances fit into two main categories. In the first category are the ones that 'drop in' from somewhere ready-made and complete, and in the second are the ones that need work. The inspiration to 'birth' a dance usually comes from the music – I hear something that just **has** to be to be danced to. Much less frequently it is the other way round; I feel a need to express something in movement and a dance will come for it, the music not until later. One dance, **Salmon**, for instance, came to life in Canada in the

102

summer of 1994 – but it was months before I heard the perfect music for it!

With the dances in the first category I have no memory afterwards of having done anything! The steps just danced through me as if the dance already existed in the ether waiting for the right music and an available body. These are the most satisfying while, paradoxically, giving me the feeling that I had nothing to do with their birth. **White Bird** comes into this category, so do **Dolphin**, **Hex**, **Return of the Unicorn**, **Between the Worlds**, **Greensleeves**, **Sunburst**, **Sacred Hoop**, **Daring**, **Salmon**, **Cloud of Unknowing**, **Vision Quest**, **Shadows**, **Fearless**, **Fire Walking**, and **Insider**.

White Bird was the first to arrive.[12] The first four steps describe the form of a bird, the Dove of peace, wings outstretched; with the remaining, travelling steps the bird flies then settles again, as if alighting on a branch. Looking at this on a subtler level – the dancer stands, at the beginning, at the centre of an equal-armed cross, and the steps first honour these four directions, looking at each and acknowledging all the strands of life from the peace of the centre. In this place of stillness everything is reconciled and integrated, and only when this is done do the steps lead out and into the world. It is the left foot that leads, so the inspiration for this moving out comes from the non-rational, intuitive centre. The steps finally come to a close and the dancer centres once more, rising and falling on the heels and settling into a moment of containment and inner peace.

I taught this dance at the Findhorn International Sacred Dance Festival at Bernhard Wosien's last visit to Britain, and a Spanish woman who was there was able to tell us what the words mean:

> *I want them to bury me*
> *Like my ancestors*
> *In the dark and cool belly*
> *Of an earthenware pot.*
>   *When life loses itself*
> *Behind a curtain of years*
> *Loves and disenchantments*
> *Will live forever*

These words felt somehow appropriate to the dance (or the dance to the words), but I couldn't quite tell why at the time, except perhaps that I recognised the theme of peace was both in the dance and in the song. In the song, it is the peace of death, meaning going beyond illusions, masks and attachments to the peace within, which matches the steps.

Circle Dancing

Pieter Brabers, a Circle Dance teacher originally from Holland, brought it all together – peace, doves and earthenware pots – in his rich and fascinating article in The Grapevine, Winter 1991/92. This is what he discovered:

> '*The Dove in ancient times was the sacred bird of the Mother Goddess, especially Aphrodite. So we have the Goddess as life **giver** – hence the sacred bird symbolising love-making (Turtle Dove), and the Goddess as life **taker** – the peace of death (Peace Dove). (I see the Dove here as the soul returning home, to the Mother.) Later, when patriarchy had taken over, the Dove became the symbol of Sophia, the feminine face of God, and still later Christianity adopted the Dove as the sign of the Holy Ghost.*
>
> *So we have two aspects of the triple Great Goddess – the Creator and the Destroyer. What of the Mother, the Preserver of life? In ancient times earthenware pots were used for two purposes, storage of food and drink (grain, seeds, oil, wine) and as grave jars for burial. The music of White Bird (Vasija de Barro) comes from Ecuador where the people have, for thousands of years, buried their dead in earthenware pots – as they have in many other places, including Greece. These pots symbolised the Mother, the Earth, the womb which contained the seeds of the harvest for the new cycle, which fed the people, and to which they returned at death to await reincarnation. So the peace of Vasija de Barro is not only the peace of death but also the peace in life from being in harmony with the natural cycles.*'

What a lot buried in an eight step dance!

Hex is another dance that dropped in ready-made from the Cosmic Choreographer. It is a dance with no hand hold but powerful arm movements which co-ordinate with the steps; on each slow beat the heel drums the off beat, which give a great feeling of strength. The style of the dance is very precise and contained; the more economical the movements the greater the energy that builds. It starts with a movement to open the heart and make space to grow; then a section to clear away impediments to growth, or rather the false notions of self which block the true self from emerging; a section connecting to this true self and the guidance from above, and finally there is integration of the various aspects of the self focussed on the 'power' centre, the hara, or Tan Tien, or sacral area in the belly. It is a dance that gives the dancer a great feeling of personal power and the ability to take charge of their lives. What is extraordinary to me is that when I heard Mari Boine Persen's amazing music my body instantly began to move to it, I just **knew** how to dance this music – I'd always known! The dance came through a dreamlike consciousness, as if I'd had a brain by-pass. A year or so later I was told the movements are the same, or very similar, to the dances of the Inuit and Sami shamans. (The singer, Mari Boine Persen, is Sami, from Northern Scandinavia). It certainly didn't come from me but rather **through** me. It seems to be possible to step aside and simply be a conduit, an earth point, and so tap into other realities, into the collective memory bank, higher consciousness or whatever. Or is it that there is a wisdom and a knowing in the body which, when the linear brain, the personality and the conditioned reflexes move out of the control room, is free to emerge, to express and create? Both I feel sure are true, probably they are the same, certainly the one interweaves with the other.

With **Dolphin**, **Salmon** and **Return of the Unicorn** I had the extraordinary experience of being danced **by** these creatures. I **was** a dolphin, a salmon, a unicorn and they gave me the dances. It was awesome to know how it feels to be a dolphin in the freedom of the ocean or a leaping salmon, and to feel their power, sleekness and muscle in my body – or mine in theirs! Quite breathtaking too to *be* a unicorn and feel that sacred white purity and joyful innocence in my body. The Salmon dance starts with the salmon free in the ocean, then in the second part it turns and pushes its way up stream so the movements are as if against a resistance, and in the final part, birth and death become two faces of the same experience as the salmon lays her eggs and quivers in death. It was breathtaking too to be a unicorn in the room in Sweden where the dance came to me. To feel that sacred white purity and joyful innocence in my body and to dance the little light prancing steps to the joyous South American music. When I teach the dance I invite the dancers to look up on the part when they move to the centre with their arm raised like the horn, and without doubt by the end of the dance a pure white unicorn will appear up there in the middle of the circle!

In the second category the dances don't just happen, they need conscious birthing; they require **work**. ('That's the right step for part A, but how can I avoid ending on the wrong foot in part B...?' etc.). The way in, however, is the same for all dances – I just let my body move to the music and feel how to express it. The left-brain will then kick in to solve the problems.

The two dances **Greensleeves** and **Shadows** came as a new departure for me, which I found exciting. They are both intensely personal in the sense that they came out of a deep need to express what was happening in me and in my life at the time. The steps for **Greensleeves** are based on courtly Elizabethan dance, and the dance came in the middle 1990s from a yearning for union. At one point in the dance the right arm lifts to the sky in an emploring gesture while the left rests on the heart where the ache for union resides. The dance from a place of isolation and separation and from a desire to reunite with – the Divine? – the Beloved? – lost parts of myself? It was certainly a cry and a dance from my soul.

Shadows in the early 1990s came out of a lengthy and tacky disentangling from a long relationship, and a time when I knew I was projecting my shadow – my inner unresolved issues – onto this former lover. Again the dancers dance individually without holding hands. It is a dance of resistance and acceptance, the arms begin by pushing away the feelings inside we don't want to acknowledge but finally the movements soften into acceptance and an awareness of inclusion. Out walking late one afternoon in bright sunlight, I began to move with my huge shadow on the grass, playing with her, rejecting her and finally accepting and embracing her. It was a moving and healing experience, as I still find the dance to be today. Recently however the 'meaning' in the dance has changed for me and the next time I taught it after this shift had happened I said nothing of its origins or meaning. At the end I asked the circle how it was for them and for each it had been a profound, but also a very personal experience. That is one of the magical things about these circle dances – the way they speak individually; their 'meaning' is not written in stone.

Finally I have found this process of birthing a dance to be organic. Push too hard and it will not be perfectly formed, it may even be still-born! If the time is not right there could be a miscarriage! So there have been long stretches of time with nothing forthcoming – like a long deep winter sleep – but then from out of the blue, or rather from out of the dark, in its own time there may come another little shoot of creativity! A dance just will not be hurried, forced or 'done', it will emerge only when the time is right and when I am ready. What a humbling process it is!

The rest I leave to Great Mystery, with gratitude for being of service in this way and for all the learning I receive from such an absorbing creative process.

18

Lines and Circles
– balancing left- and right-brain

'There's no straight lines make up my life and all my roads have bends.'

Harry Chapin

On a deep level, and put simplistically and baldly, what we are doing in Sacred/Circle Dance is re-creating balance between masculine energy and feminine energy, between the circle and the line. I find it interesting and significant that both Circle and Line Dancing are currently popular forms. For wholeness, however, lines and circles need to come together; each is incomplete without the other!

As we have seen, humanity has journeyed from a circle consciousness to a patriarchal, line consciousness, and now circle consciousness is returning. However, life spirals forward and upward, and there is, literally, no future in attempting to turn the clock back to re-create the circle life as it was pre-patriarchy; that is backward looking in a non-productive sense, a denial of the Life Force, and ends anyway in a cul-de-sac. Circle consciousness on its own is no longer sufficient, any more than exclusive focus on the feminine is sufficient or appropriate.

William Blake speaks of the journey we make from innocence through experience and back to innocence. But it is not a return to a blind, ignorant innocence: from the experience gained we move into a wiser, more aware, and consciously chosen innocence. In other words we have experienced and absorbed the gifts of the 'masculine', we have experienced and integrated the energy of the 'line', which is the energy that gives perspective, and the ability and the responsibility to make choices.

The revolution that happened in the 'love and light' explosion of the 1960s, which saw the feminine rising to challenge 'negative' patriarchal values, like Botticelli's Venus emerging from the waves, set the stage

107

for the eventual restoration of balance between masculine and feminine. But with all swings of the pendulum there is the danger of going too far in the opposite direction. And as with all pendulum swings the centre point of balance will eventually be found. The balance this time will come through masculine consciousness.

Water bursting its banks goes nowhere, and some of this feminine energy from the 1960s went nowhere in the sense that it was wishy-washy, airy and ungrounded. There is no sense attempting to return to the undifferentiated feminine, to the dreamlike tribal oneness of our ancestors, to the innocence of the original circle: what is needed now is to bring the circle and the line together.

Let's look in greater depth at this polarity of line and circle. There is a different impact on our senses from a circular room and a square room with its lines and edges, between a circle of people and a line of people in a queue, or soldiers in a platoon; between desks lined up in rows and a circle of cushions on the floor.

Circles have neither a beginning nor an ending. They symbolise the sun, the moon and the earth, the womb and The Great Mother. They invoke and celebrate the greater circles – the cycle of the seasons, the cycle of life and the wheel of death and rebirth. Circles stand for wholeness. In a circle all are equal, no one is more important or in front of anyone; there is an intimacy in a circle; circles are about connecting and relating; they flow you, hold and embrace you. They create a unity between the dancers facing one another. Wherever you are in the circle you can see everyone else and you are always in direct communication with the centre, with the Source.

In a line however there is a beginning and an ending, a past, a present and a future. A line moves directly forward focused on a goal so a leader is implicit. It speaks of the military, authority, hierarchy. A line states that communication is unimportant but what is important is getting to the goal; there is no face to face connection, the view ahead is someone's else's back and the focus is the task. In a line you look forward, in a circle you look around. Line consciousness without the softening of a circle is the energy of the corporate world, which is rapidly concentrating power, destroying the natural world, and siphoning off the planet's wealth into a few greedy pockets.

The Czechoslovak writer Milan Kundera in '*The Book of Laughter and Forgetting*' tells of a picture in a weekly news magazine in which a row of men in uniform with guns and with Plexiglas vizors are watching casually dressed young people dancing in a circle. '*They feel the circle they describe is a magic circle bonding them in a ring.*' It's clearly a time just before a confrontation. There on one side are the gloomy police in their official ranks, in their *'imposed unity'*, facing on the other side the joyful young people united in the *'organic unity'* of their dancing circle.

So what of the image of the cross and the circle? This is an ancient symbol for the sun, the spirit, coming into matter, the earth. The hot cross bun with the marzipan or pastry cross on the top comes from ancient 'goddess' buns symbolising the 'mother' taking the 'son'/'sun' back into herself as the mother earth takes the sun back into herself each night and each winter. A cross could possibly be seen as a symbol of division and conflict but when contained within a circle it tells of the reconciling of opposites, and the harmonious bringing together of energies.

The two energies, 'male' and 'female', move through each human body in the pattern of the Caduceus. The Caduceus, which represents the flow of subtle energies both in the human body and in the body of the earth, is an ancient glyph of two serpents rising, intertwined, around the staff of Hermes. According to the myth, when Hermes threw his staff between two fighting snakes the snakes stopped fighting and coiled up the staff together. So the Caduceus, being an expression of integration, balance and harmony, became the symbol of some medical groups.

The Caduceus symbolises the power that is channelled when polarity energies are brought into balance and focused. In the body, the staff is seen as the spine and the snakes represent the two currents that

A Caduceus, emblem of Hermes, the messenger of the gods, and the glyph of some medical bodies.

flow up in spirals around it. These currents are known as Ida and Pingala, and are governed by, respectively, the moon and the sun. They twine around the spine and rise through the body to meet in the head bringing insight and illumination.

In the slaying of the Minotaur at the centre of the Cretan labyrinth (an act which can be seen as the releasing of creative energy), these two energies combine, and the co-operation of both is needed to redeem this hidden demon and transform it into creative power. It takes both a Theseus and an Ariadne, the dancing together of intuition and will, the straight and direct sword thrust as well as the winding ball of thread, to do the deed.

In the space between dark and light, where Theseus and Ariadne, the vision of spirit and the soul of the earth, meet and harmonise; in the brain where Ida and Pingala fuse; in the centre point where the two circles of the Vesica Pisces interlock, there are no opposites, no light or dark, simply the pure state of Being.

The spiral is the form of the DNA molecule, the basic key pattern or map of life, thus the Caduceus shows life overcoming death. The staff or sword represents the will, which can hold the untamed earth energy, the lower self, and transmute it into a higher vibration.

Such energy lines are also present in the earth. Across the lower half of England, bisecting the land from East Anglia to Cornwall, run two lines of contrasting energy linking some of the most powerful ancient sites in the country. They are known as the Michael and Mary lines. St. Michael, the bearer of the sword of light, who clears the way for the awakening of humanity to its true nature, is in intimate dance with the Earth goddess in her guise as Mary.

These two energies function inside each of us with a greater or lesser degree of balance. Do we run our lives like a well-captained ship, planning every detail and bowing daily to the gods of time keeping and efficiency? Do we 'go with the flow', wait and see what happens, leave everything to the 'universe' or the 'higher powers' or whatever? We need line energy, it can get us somewhere; but it also needs to be exposed to circle energy to keep the journey oriented to the centre. We need circle consciousness but without the integrity of the line every-thing stays the same as it has always been and life goes round and round getting nowhere.

Sacred/Circle Dance is not exempt from this possibility. A familiar circle is a very safe and relaxing place to be. For some new dancers it may be the first place they have ever experienced such safety and relaxation. They sink gratefully into an atmosphere that affirms them and allows them to be themselves. It's wonderful to see tension slip away and the true beauty of the spirit begin to emerge. But safe harbours are intended to be temporary resting places not permanent residences. The atmosphere of security and loving affirmation that the circle provides can become such a bewitching comfort zone that the seas may no longer be challenged. The line must intersect the circle here so that life not only rotates but also goes forward. The undifferentiated 'feminine' is not a healthy place in which to get stuck.

Sacred/Circle dancers are predominantly female. Since it is fundamentally the energy of the feminine that is being grounded through the Dance it is natural that women feel more drawn to it: it is affirming and empowering to reconnect with the power and support of 'sisterhood' and to have your true nature validated publicly. But the issue in question, whether in a male or a female body, is balance.

For some women who have been poured into a masculine mould and have an over developed orientation to goals, achieving and intellect, coming to the Dance is like arriving at an oasis in the desert! They will drink deep and immerse themselves to find the balance they need for wholeness. The same is true for men with a top-heavy animus. For both men and women with an already strong 'feminine', however, it is the quest on the high seas, the energy of the line that is needed for wholeness. This is on the level of gender, personality and physical energy.

On the spiritual level, the reason for seeking balance and wholeness is to bring one's spirit home, or to come home to one's spirit, which is genderless! This is the ultimate purpose of the Dance for the individual. There is also a wider planetary purpose, which we have looked at earlier in the section on S.E.E.D.

That the effect of power in the hands of the 'negative' masculine is causing imbalance on the earth is undeniable. We witness daily the destruction caused by this linear power. It is clear from a higher perspective that the positive qualities of the 'feminine' – the nurturing, the compassion, the forgiving; the all embracing and receptive; the quality of stillness; the ability to hold the truth within and live from that – are needed to transform our world. This is what we have been holding and continue to hold for the earth and for humanity in our dancing circles. But on its own, even all of that is not enough! For true healing there has to be a reuniting with the true masculine, the 'god' must return and dance with the 'goddess'.

I have said earlier that circles 'keep things as they are'; this is due to their inward focus and the fact that they can only move around where they are; they go up and down at times, but always on the same spot.

However, this is not true of a conscious **dancing** circle! What happens when a circle starts to turn is that the energy begins to spiral. Any circular movement in the space/time dimension becomes a spiral, as it is impossible to return to the same place in time. It remains within the same horizontal dimension but is free to move inwards and outwards, and up and down in its spiral form.

From the perspective of the circle on the ground the movement of the spiral is to the right. This is the direction that the vast majority of Sacred/Circle dances move in. However, as a physical body moving through space displaces air, it automatically creates a stream of energy going in the opposite direction. Let a car race past you as you laboriously pedal home on your bike, or overtake a huge lorry in your little car on the motorway and you'll know all about this energy stream.

These vortices of energy moving in opposite directions, one travelling up, the other, down, operate in dancing circles. They connect the earth with the cosmos through the dancers, both raising the energy of the earth and at the same time grounding cosmic energy. Though the circle is physically limited to the spot where it dances, its effect is far-reaching: the energy of the circle radiates out – like a stone dropped into water sending ripples out as far as the eye can see.

19

Alignment and Atunement
– the energetic structure of the Dance circle

> *'The place of the Dance, whether it seems to be a sacred shrine or the unclean burning ground of the corpse, is, in reality, the human heart.'*
>
> One of the legends of Shiva's dance

Weighed down under a mountain of equipment – heavy music system, mood setting paraphernalia including soft pink table lamp, flowering pot plant, bags of crystals, sarongs and floaty coloured scarves, rolls of workshop leaflets, current Grapevines, a clock, and a torch (for when the evening draws to a quiet, meditative candlelit close and the music player disappears into the shadows), travelling iron and brown paper (as wax on carpets is an occupational hazard), candlestick under one arm and incense sticks coming out of the ears, the Sacred/Circle Dance teacher arrives equipped and ready to transform some dingy, strip-lit vibe-free hall into a Temple of Dance!

Dance spaces benefit from a physical as well as an energetic cleanse, so the feet of the dancers don't pick up old stuff. Amazingly even a floor that appears clean will yield dirt if it's simply wiped with a damp cloth tied around a broom. The teacher/focaliser not only changes the physical environment into a place of fragrant beauty: ordinary space is transformed into sacred space by the intent of the atunement. There are many ways for the individual dancers to come into unity within sacred space before the dancing begins: this is a choice for the teacher/focaliser. It is often done by silence. What is important is the intent, and it is for the teacher to know and hold the intent and bring the dancers into that prepared focused place.

I very slightly altered the following poem of Bernhard's – (sacrilege!) – to make it into an invocation for the beginning of the dancing:

> *'You who move the universe move me also*
> *Take me out of the depths and lift me high to yourself*
> *I dance the song of stillness*
> *Setting my foot to the music of the cosmos*
> *I lift my dance to the heavens*
> *And feel your smile blessing me.'*
>
> What I changed – *'Setting'* on line four to *'Set'*;
> – *'I lift'* to *'And lift'*; and
> – *'And feel'* to *'Till I feel'*

In the early days, the beginning of the 1980s, we got quite pompous and flowery at times when 'atuning' the circles! Past lives as priests and priestesses were being reactivated, I feel, as we found ourselves once again in a leading role invoking the divine in sacred space. *'Lord and Lady of the Dance'* was a favourite, *'The Cosmic Dancer'* was my own number one, and *'Terpsichore'* really raised energy and eyebrows! I blush at all this now, especially Terpsichore!

The Dance is for everyone, and when the name was changed from *Sacred* Dance to *Circle* Dance it was opened up for everyone to feel included. We wanted to avoid alienating and excluding anyone; and as there were those who felt they had exclusive rights on the word 'sacred', and others who had had uncomfortable past experiences of professional 'sacredness', or who feared dogma or 'preachiness', calling it simply Circle Dance made it more universally available. This was all very laudable, but having done that, to **then** invoke a Greek muse, to call on Terpsichore! Guaranteed to fragment unity and divide the circle into 'them that knows' and 'them that don't'! It felt right at the time though, and these things have evolved, as we have.

As all things have a beginning, middle and end, and energy follows thought, the intent at the beginning of a Dance session is clearly crucial to what follows – it sets the stage and prepares the appropriate space. What I now do to start is an energy alignment, an atunement that connects line energy with the circle and build an energetic light temple. It puts the dancers and the circle into a larger perspective, connecting them to the earth, the cosmos, each other, all beings, and to all the kingdoms of nature. Generally I speak this aloud to bring it into everyone's consciousness.

So the first awareness is of the still centre within the individual dancer.

Then comes the alignment of the individual on the vertical axis; this line moves down through the body to the centre of the earth: this is grounding, and releases any apprehension, giving the dancer a feeling of security. The line then travels back through the body and up to the sun, to align with the higher worlds.

Next comes the horizontal axis; this line runs around the circle; travelling from the heart down the left arm into the palm and heart of the person on the left as it comes in via the right palm. At once there is a clear union of vertical linear energy with flowing and undulating horizontal circle energy.

Then comes a third linear link – a line coming from behind, passing through the heart and on into the heart of the circle. This connects the circle with the great circle of life bringing in all beings, creatures and kingdoms of nature. In addition (though this is not referred to in the atunement), there are the luminous threads, or fibres as they are sometimes called, coming from the body connecting us with all life on the planet and beyond. Lastly there is the focus on the still point at the centre of the circle, the Source, the '*still centre*' where as T.S. Eliot says, '*the Dance is*'! Together all these lines create a dynamic energy temple in which to dance; they put the circle in the context of creation and enable the energy which will build during the dancing to affect the whole, positively.

The pattern is beautiful and always suffused with light. One cone sits on top of the other making a diamond shape: the apex of the top cone is the centre of the sun, and of the lower the centre of the earth, and the middle of this diamond shape is dissected by a line of light. Seen three-dimensionally the temple has as many sides as there are dancers, likewise radiating lines of light. And in this sacred space we dance.

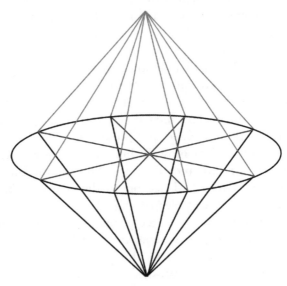

Diagram of etheric Dance
Temple. By Esbjorn Aneer.

20

Women Leading
– why women are now leading creative spiritual change

> '*The Goddess is re-emerging today as a change-maker, restoring balance, wholeness and peace by reconnecting us with Nature, our innate wisdom, and the sacredness of all life.*'
>
> '*Amulets of the Goddess*'
> Nancy Blair

I am often asked 'Why are Sacred/Circle Dance circles predominantly women? Where are the **men**?' Men are a minute minority – maybe a couple in a circle of twenty, sometimes not even one. There still seems to be a thought form in civilised western society that dancing is something women do, that men who dance are effeminate, not **real** men! Men do football and rock climbing and wrestling; women paint their nails, go shopping and dance. In the European countries that still have clear links to their cultural past such as Greece, Turkey and Russia, both the men and the women dance; sometimes together at festivals and weddings and so on, but the men also dance on their own, as do the women. The men dance the strong warrior and hunting dances, dances of male pride and protection.

One of my most thrilling dance experiences was in Athens watching a line of Pontic men from the shores of the Black Sea (in what is now an area of Greece), dance on to the stage of the open air Dora Stratou theatre.[14] It was electrifying. They moved as one unit, they vibrated with passion, they were invincible; they embodied the powerful essence of the masculine; the god had entered them, and was dancing them. (I have also seen this dancing god quality in two dancers, apart from Bernhard Wosien – David Roberts, Switzerland and Erik

116

Bendix, America, I see it in my partner Esbjorn practising Gatka, the Sikh martial art with swords.) I remember the time Bernhard announced at Findhorn that he would teach a Tsamikos but that as it was a man's dance only the men were to dance it! I remember too, that once I had expressed and got over my anger at such 'old-fashioned macho' behaviour, how exciting it was to watch the men shedding 'nice' Englishness and come into their masculine power. I would have no anger at such a thing now; part of reclaiming true human birthright is for men to have the space to explore with other man what is uniquely male, and for women to explore true femininity with other women.

For the majority of northern men to dance, a cultural barrier has first to be overcome. There are some acceptably male forms such as Morris dancing, and now Line dancing and Salsa are making dance more readily available to men, but the appeal of these two is strongly social and sexual, you probably wouldn't go to a Salsa evening for an uplifting or spiritual experience! I would say that Sacred/Circle Dance has all three – it can be a social, sensual and spiritual experience, and can be, as for example in the Rom/Gypsy dances, a sexual one too. A major healing factor in Sacred/Circle Dance is that it glues separate pieces together again. For example in the past I have very much needed the energy of the 'male' dances, such as Tsamikos. They have played a big part in my healing and balancing and helped me to find and integrate my inner 'masculine' strength.

As consciousness rises and science backs up what is being experienced, the division between material and spiritual, between sacred and profane, is dissolving. Earth is now recognised as a living being imbued with spirit and is frequently referred to by her Greek goddess name, Gaia. Quantum Physics can now prove as 'fact' what we have long felt – that trees, rocks, water are materialised spirit. Everything is perceived as being alive, even the body of a dead animal or a rotting compost heap are far from dead: they are full of life busily transforming the old form into a new one. Everything is imbued with spirit, everything has life – there is no opposite of life (it certainly isn't death; if there has to be an opposite, birth would fit!). This re-union of spirit and matter happens as a direct body experience in Sacred/Circle Dance.

Then there is the historical perspective: a male system has been running things on this planet for centuries, women have been considered inferior, appendages and possessions of men, and even as their *'goods and chattels'*. Now there is a re-balancing and the feminine spirit is in the ascendant and as, generally speaking, women contain a greater degree of femininity than men, it is mainly women who are spearheading the change.

Finally there is the spiritual dimension. Neuropsychologist James Prescott at the Institute of Humanistic Science reports that women have unique neural links between their forebrain and their cerebellum, between, in effect, their physical bodies and the spiritual planes. These links mean that sensations of physical pleasure go directly to the neocortex or higher brain centre and are integrated there. Apparently men do not have these connections. Women moved from primate sexuality with its oestrus cycle to a menstrual cycle and developed a sexuality that is not only for reproduction but also for bonding and affection. Thus, the researchers maintain, women need to lead *'towards the integration of the conscious and unconscious mind and to a more profound understanding of the spiritual nature of the species'*.

Could it be that the reason the single all powerful and all embracing divinity (who was female), and her worship (which lasted for at least 22,000 years) – was crushed and replaced with a creation myth casting women as evil, sexual temptresses was precisely because of the spiritual power of women? And could it also be that the swing to the patrirchal rule of the past 3000 or so years has been a necessary stage of our under-standing in order that true balance may be established.

Some women experience orgasm so intensely that they go through the veil and enter a state of altered consciousness, experiencing a flash of spiritual enlightenment. I can confirm this having experienced it myself. In this ecstatic and intense orgiastic state it is possible for matter and spirit to fuse in the woman, and it is this fusion, this oneness of the physical and the spiritual, that is at the heart of all mystical experience.

This means that merging with the divine can happen through the body, so an intermediary such as a priest is not necessary; it means that women are, through their bodies, natural 'priestesses', and that through the powerful energy of sacred sex a woman can touch the divine and open the way for the man to follow. This is not to say that men cannot touch the divine this way too, there are practices in the Tantric tradition to facilitate this for both men and women.

This power is the reason women were denigrated and sex was split from spirituality. Women **had** to be presented as evil and sex as dirty and sinful – the convenient myth of Eve the temptress creating the split – so that the patriarchy, which feared their power, could control them and allow the filtering of spirituality to come only through the male created religions.

Originally there was no split between matter and spirit, body and soul, sacred and secular, and we are gradually finding our way back to that wholeness. It appears that men do not have these particular neural connections, so this could be one reason why it is natural that women are now leading on the journey towards spiritual understanding and wholeness. The pendulum swings and this time the women are the initiators, bringing back the values of the old matriarchal world and pioneering the way into the age of freedom and truth.

Or coming full circle? Women have always danced, as have men, and always honoured the circle as far back, we know, as paleolithic times[15] as can be seen in cave paintings of that time. It is said there is nothing new under the sun!

21

Other Dimensions
– the interaction through the Dance with other levels of being

'Could there be anything more blessed
Than to imitate on earth
The ring dance of the angels?'

St Basil
4th century Bishop of Caesarea

The hind brain, which is separated from the forebrain by the midbrain, is located at the junction of the spinal cord and cerebrum. This region contains the more primitive structures of the brain from an evolutionary standpoint, but they function to regulate some of the most vital processes in the body. Breathing, heart rate, and muscle coordination are controlled here and sensory impulses are filtered and routed at this point.

The cerebellum is the most ancient part of the brain. It controls our primary survival instinct also our balance and muscle co-ordination. A useful organ for dancers! In the much larger part of the brain however, the fore brain or cerebrum, is the cerebral cortex, the region where most of the higher processes such as memory, logical thought, consciousness, and reasoning are carried out and where we connect to Source, to higher mind and therefore to our highest potential. These two parts may be called the lower and higher brain, and they connect to the lower and higher aspects of the self. Electromagnetic energy fields from the moon and sun, planets and the stars are constantly bathing the earth, and the cerebrum has developed in order to cope with this. It filters this powerful cosmic energy and makes it available for us on a physical human day-to-day level.

We have an energy body separate but intermingling with the physical one. In fact we have several. Energy, i.e. Life Force or Chi or

Ki in eastern traditions, permeates every atom, molecule and cell within the physical body. In martial arts the Chi or Ki is extended and directed at will and it is this energy body that defeats the opponent. This Chi or Ki can become blocked and acupuncture and shiatsu work on clearing the flow of these energy lines within the body to facilitate healing. It is possible with practice and focus to become aware of the etheric energy within the body and to directly experience the self as indestructible and immortal. We will see the power of this energy at work later in this chapter in the description of the fire dancers in the Bulgarian mountains.

According to Druid and Mayan and other shamanic traditions, we have a network of millions of luminous fibres extending from our toes and fingers, fine threads from our bodies extending into the past and on into the future, connect us into the great web of all life. So we have an all-time link with the cosmos and the higher part of ourselves, with the fully enlightened ones we in truth are; we also have links with time past, time future, all actions and all life on the planet.

Don Juan describes these fibres of light to Castaneda as looking like white cobwebs, luminous and bristling out in all directions and putting us in touch with all things. When a dancing circle is aligned, energy from above, energy from the earth and from all the kingdoms of nature flows into the circle along these fibres, and energy from the dance flows out along them. As our arms don't end at the finger tips, nor our feet at the points of our toes, and our energy body continues on and on without end, the dancing affects everyone, and the circle holds everything within it.

We are each the centre of a web and have access to all dimensions, and the doors of perception of the world behind this material one can be opened by spiritual or shamanic practices. Our true 'seeing' has been reduced to a three-dimensional picture of reality, but at certain times the veil may dissolve and we then can see clearly and access the higher reality.

I frequently 'see' or have a fleeting awareness of whoever first taught me a dance as I begin to pass it on to a circle. This only happens when the dance was so embodied by that teacher that dance and dancer were inseparable, when I experienced that the dancer was being danced by that dance, and **became** that dance. This is the magic, this flow of truth through the pores of the body, soul speaking to soul of the essence of existence.

John Perkins in his book *Shapeshifting* writes

> '*You have to accept that you already **are** the same as the thing that you are going to shift into – that your separateness is only an illusion. You must also believe that there is no hierarchy, that you as human*

being are no higher on some evolutionary chart than you as tree or jaguar.'

Likewise we have to accept that we are no lower than the angels, than the 'gods' and 'goddesses'! The Dance can create a doorway to the spirit world, and bring the gods and goddesses before us. I have experienced this doorway many times in Dance events, instances when the veil of perception has lifted and the Unmanifest has been visible. When the conditions have been right, the energy pure and focussed, the circle clear, lo and behold, the curtain opens and there, for instance, is the discarnate Bernhard in all his glory, the overlighting angel of the Dance. *'Who was that in the centre of the circle at the end?'*, a clairvoyant friend asked me in hushed tones. *'Oh that's Bernhard. He pops in all the time!' 'I thought so'* she replied with a knowing look.

During a residential 'Danceshop' in Oxfordshire which was a celebration of Beltane, the beginning of summer in the Celtic year and the time of union and blossoming, we were holding the energy after a particularly powerful dance, which had left the whole circle vibrating. I became aware of a vast and utterly beautiful being filling the circle – an angel presence – and realised with a shock of recognition that it was the Spirit of Beltane!

To say it was a surprise sounds naïve, but even after so many years of working with the festivals it hadn't really dawned on me that each one is over lighted by, or *is*, in some magical way, a living Spirit, a Devic Being. The feeling I had from the 'Angel' was that dancing and celebrations actually help these Beings grow and evolve. It was both a humbling and an empowering experience.

Many years ago, I started, as part of weekend Danceshops, the tradition of the Saturday 'whites' ceremonial evening. Ceremony creates a sacred space in which actions that are performed in the physical sphere give power inwardly to the soul, and affect our lives. The room is candlelit for these ceremonies and everyone wears white (or around the winter solstice, black or very dark). This helps to create an atmosphere in which the lower brain and everyday reality can be transcended.

Occasionally at the end of particularly powerful Saturday evening ceremonies during residential weekends I have felt myself filled by a huge presence I can only describe as divine. My body became pure electric energy; I couldn't have moved if I'd wanted to so awesome were these experiences. Dancers would come and stand in front of me, looking in silence, and I knew they could see the energy I was feeling. I knew they were seeing and honouring the energy of the Divine

Feminine, and recognising it as themselves. I felt afterwards that some 'goddess' energy must have come in and taken over my body, and wondered who it would have been. Now I suspect it was probably me, the divine goddess-Me that is. It doesn't really matter what name it is given. I recount this in order to give an example of the Reality behind physical form, to show that this transcendant realm can be accessed by anyone, as it is in fact who we are, and how the Dance can create an environment conducive to the thinning of the veil between the physical and spiritual dimensions.

I witnessed this phenomenon happening to another woman one summer during a weekend in Canada. On this occasion we weren't indoors and it wasn't even at night. It was the last morning – the Sunday morning – we were dancing on the grass in the sun and reviewing a dance that had become very special to the circle over the weekend. It's called **Joc de la Sinzienne**, a Romanian harvest dance. I had spoken the day before of how it is believed that, traditionally, the women danced this naked with garlands of flowers,[17] while the men were 'off stage'. The music starts with the women calling and then the men are heard shouting in celebration.

One of the women was missing from our circle that morning. I knew what was going to happen – she had asked me earlier, but I was in no way prepared for what **did** happen. We started to dance and suddenly, as if from the ethers, a goddess appeared; a breathtakingly beautiful, naked goddess, carrying an armful of flowers; she was translucent, glowing with star dust; she walked, glided rather, into the circle as we danced – a vision of spirit in our midst – laid the flowers in the centre and gracefully slipped away.

It lasted a few seconds only but was an experience of eternity. I don't think there was a dry eye in that circle as we ended the dance and stood in reverent silence. If there was, it was because it had been too profound for tears. It touched us deep in our souls, cracked our defences and opened us all to love and a knowing of our true nature.

By embodying the 'goddess' she showed us who we are, she mirrored back to us the light that radiates through us when we dance, the light we are while still in mortal bodies.

In 1938 folk dancer Philip Thornton (see endnote [1], page 153) visited Bulgaria to experience the Fire Walking Ritual by the Nestinari in the village of Bulgari. This was performed to bring fertility and health to the region (until it was outlawed by the communist government in 1960[16]). Only the Nestinari women danced; they had to be either widows or virgins and must have attended confession that morning.

No man was permitted to dance into the fire on pain of sudden death.

On this one specific day of the year, very close to Midsummer, two ikons, said to be miracle workers, were brought to the village square from their secret chapel in the woods. A wood pile five feet high, covering an area twenty feet by twenty feet, was built while hundreds of dancers were dancing a local dance to the music of Bulgarian bagpipes. They danced for an hour, the music then stopped, and two priests, accompanied by two other people carrying the ikons, walked around the pile.

The fire was then lit and in silence the huge crowd watched it burn until there was a mass of white hot charcoal eighteen inches deep around the flames. The heat was tremendous. The ikon bearers walked around the fire once more then the musicians began the rhythmic dance music again, and two women came forward, were blessed by the priests; they kissed the ikons and danced before them.

Their eyes rolled up under their lids and their faces were set in a sublime smile as they then took the ikons and holding them in front of them danced straight into the flames. They danced three times across and three times round the fire on the white hot ashes holding the large ikons. According to Philip Thornton their trailing black dresses were unsinged and the naked feet of both women were smooth, soft and unmarked, without even a blister. A watching gendarme said as he crossed himself, '*This is a miracle of God*'.

I have danced some of these ritual fire walking dances for a prolonged time and after twenty, thirty minutes or so I have felt, yes I could walk into the fire now! I have felt, at least, I understand how it is possible to enter such a heightened state through the Dance that the restrictions of normal reality can be transcended and it is possible to dance through the veil. This is total surrender to the Dance!

There are, thankfully, some things we cannot understand with our minds; we may theorise and analyse and dissect what the Dance is about and how it works and all the levels and effects of it, but a dimension eludes us, as it does with the fire dance of the Nestinari. Let it be as Jesus said to the disciples when he danced with them before the crucifixion – '*I will that it be called a mystery*'.

22

Money, Dance and Love
– value for value, and the higher significance of money

> *'Money is like manure; it's not worth a thing unless it's spread around encouraging young things to grow.'*
>
> *'The Matchmaker'*
> Thornton Wilder

The issue of money has created a tug-of-war within me over the years. How I now see the issue of this internal battle is that it is about self worth. My childhood family survived on the mean stipend (the very word sounds mean!) from my father's church; my parents were constantly trying to *'make ends meet!'* – turning a line into a circle? – and I inherited a strong foundation in poverty consciousness and a fear of there never being enough. On top of this, by the time my parents and the education system had finished with me I was – well let's just say I didn't graduate with a First in Self Esteem! I learnt the shame lesson as a child; I learnt I just wasn't good enough; it was a hopeless aspiration anyway – Jesus was far too high up that wall!

Given the background it's hardly surprising that when I began to share the Dance I tucked what I called 'my begging bowl' to the side of the door; I'd quietly say it was there, if anyone felt like putting anything in, blah blah...! Sometimes I couldn't even manage to mention it at all, despite the fact that the hall needed paying for. I had learnt that harsh lesson of humility so well I was ashamed to ask for money for what I was giving.

But at the other end of the rope, pulling against these realities, was my resilient spirit and, despite everything, the tiny belief – no, the **knowing** – that somewhere very deep down inside I **was** OK and in

125

fact actually worth quite a lot. The resultant journey with self worth and money has been a great learning, and still is. What a challenge to turn all that conditioning around, and what a gift to have been engulfed in such a strong myth that I had to draw on all my inner resources to re-write it. Freedom is only truly appreciated after experiencing a prison cell. So, thanks parents!

Some Old Doubts and Fears concerning asking value for value! If I ask for good money for what I do:

- I'll meet criticism; – '*Big head!*' or my childhood put down: '*Too big for your boots*',
- I'll meet scorn; – '*Who does she think she is?*' etc.,
- I'll have to give value for it and what if I can't,
- Too much will be expected of me.

Conclusion – it's much easier, safer and more comfortable to stay hidden, and to sidle out a begging bowl.

Then one day I saw it from another angle – it wasn't really about **me**, it was about the Dance; it was the **Dance** that needed to be valued! Then my ego settled into a healthier perspective and I could ask for money in exchange for the gift of the Dance and then, eventually, also for me, being the vehicle, after all, through which it was being made available that evening or that day.

I was so fired by this revelation I wrote a short bit on it in the Spring 1989 edition of Grapevine but was hung, drawn and quartered for it in the next issue! Traditionally people who did spiritual work, the letter said, never worked for payment. Guilt! I shot underground again. I'd put my head above the parapet but it was still too dangerous to get up and speak what I felt.

The more I value the Dance and I value myself and what I give through and in the Dance, the easier it is for me to put that out in the price for the events I run. Constant tests and challenges come up over this, of course!

A recent one had me whirling backwards into that old reality for a short while, but in a matter of a day, helped by supportive friends, I came through on the value test. A friend in Canada had come across an exquisite painting of earth beings dancing in a circle and something twanged inside me. There it is, the perfect logo for what I do in the Dance – the joyful circle and the earth/Faerie connection. My friend enquired about this possibility from the artist, Una Woodruff, and was passed on to her agent who told us the price to use it would be £279! Well that's that I thought, feeling hugely disappointed. The friend said she'd have

The picture by Una Woodruff.

a go at getting it down as it was going to be used to spread the Dance and not for financial gain, but the price remains £279! Of **course** it does!

I felt great joy when I 'got' what it was about and accepted it. It was teaching me again to follow what I feel to be right, whatever the cost! And, bonus, it gives me an opportunity to give the kind of exchange I myself have been seeking by supporting this wonderful artist who has graciously mirrored me to myself.

It's a tricky area, charging for the Dance. The vast majority of circles are led by people who get their bread and butter elsewhere and teach the Dance in their spare time; for a small handful of us, however, it is our sole livelihood. At times I feel I would like to offer the Dance as my gift to people and the earth, and set a fee only to cover expenses leaving the rest to donations – or not, because there's always the possibility there wouldn't be any! Each time I suggest this to the people who set up the Danceshops, I'm met with horror! *No please, we're not ready for that!* This is an ongoing substratum to my journey with money, though, and keeps popping up for review.

Ironically, or paradoxically, here I am, at the same time, busily putting out loud and clear that I require more money in exchange for what I give through the Dance! I get such reward, such payment, just doing this stuff, but the key word is exchange. It doesn't have to be money; there are other ways apart from money to effect a satisfactory exchange, but there does have to be an exchange. I've had some wonderful experiences with alternative exchanges. They're fine provided that the bills can still be paid. The life my partner and I now enjoy has been scaled down to the bone; we live a rural life in Spain and live lightly, but it still costs money to travel to the dance events and to maintain and update equipment and so on!

Several years ago I noticed a poster for a day workshop that really appealed to me. I checked the date, yes, I was free; checked the place, yes, easy to get to; checked the price and it was free and I noticed an immediate shut off inside myself. It no longer had the appeal. Why would that be I wondered? My first reaction was – *if it doesn't cost anything it can't be worth going to. If they don't value what they're doing enough to ask for an exchange, I don't think I'd value it either.* I also look at workshops that are priced way off the planet, but the subtle message I get there is – *Ooh, this is good, this is the tops; you'd better be there; sell something, borrow the money – it's worth it!*

Why then is there a feeling of poverty consciousness in the Sacred/Circle Dance world? It's an ongoing puzzlement. Some Possible Explanatory Theories:

- Ceilidhs are cheap, what's the difference?
- Other dance classes and events are priced low, how come if it's called a 'Workshop' it costs a lot?
- It's so easy, anyone can do it, nothing to it!

The skill of a teacher is in **making** it easy. The better you are at it, the easier it seems! The Dance is available to anyone, anyone can come in, off the streets or whatever, and dance, and anyone **can** do it! A 'professional' teacher of anything aims to facilitate, and does not display what goes into what they do, any more than you want to know about the blood, sweat and tears behind getting most theatre productions on to the stage. Dancers show up for the event and the room is clean and beautiful, the music ready, the Dance Temple created, the teacher prepared in every way. No one needs to know the work behind all this. If the dancing is so well taught that the dancer dances effortlessly and joyfully they may think, '*This is easy, why should I be expected to pay good money for it?*' and they may think too '*If even I can do it, it can't be worth that much.*'

It's a question of re-creating the circle of money. For it to be healthy energy – and money is simply energy in a material form – it needs to be in a continuous flow. For the Spirit of Money to evolve it must be connected into the heart, the great spiritual organ of giving and receiving and transforming. Money is the energy of love and if we love money we spread the energy of love wherever and whenever we buy anything.

The Deva or Angel of Money is a neutral being; as Shakespeare says
– '*there is nothing good or bad but thinking makes it so*', likewise with money.
Money is sacred if that is our intent. We don't know the journey that the
money in our purse right now has been on, through which hating as well
as loving hands it has passed, how many salacious deals it may have
energised, as well as joy it may have brought, but whatever its
journey, when it comes to us it can be changed by our intent and
passed on as loving and positive creative energy. Giving £279 to Una
Woodruff will finance her to develop and spread her work and create
more inspirational paintings. Giving generously for the Dance increases
the flow of Dance energy helping the Dance grow and spread.

23

White Magic
– subtle energy at work in the Dance

> *'In the sacred dance we mirror the microcosmic order of the heavens, the gyratory movements representing the whirling of the fixed stars above the fixed earth. As we wind we create within ourselves a still centre and apprehend the power of the universe into being. As we unwind, we turn our spirit back to its divine source.'*
>
> *'The Celtic Arts Source Book'*
> Courtney Davis

What we are dealing with in **conscious** Sacred/Circle Dance is the highest form of white magic. I remember years ago being privileged to look at a couple of old books from the 1920s, which were being kept under lock and key to minimise decay. They were full of drawings, which were received by a woman clairvoyant and written down, in incredible detail, by her friend. They purport to be choreographies from the dance temples of ancient Egypt and ancient India. The lines, some in colour, swirled across the pages, sometimes crossing and re-crossing. I tried to make recognisable patterns out of them, find something with a familiar form, but failed: they were beyond such encapsulating. At the sides of the pages was minute writing giving precise instruction on the position of a foot or even the angle or tilt of a joint of a little finger. I spent a couple of hours entranced and in awe, feeling myself back there in time dancing these sacred dances.

Next day I returned to the family I was staying with in the west of England and slept that night in the elder son's room as he was away for the weekend. I could not believe my eyes – open on his desk was a sketch-book with swirls and lines that were identical to the ones I had seen in the books the day before, some were in colour others not. Time stood still. I found it hard to breathe as I went downstairs and asked his mother if she

Sacred dance. Photo by kind permission of Friedl Kloke.

knew what they were. Oh yes, she did! Sketches for Eurythmy! I was covered in goose pimples!

Eurythmy is a movement form intuited by mystic Rudolph Steiner, the founder of Anthroposophy, in the early 20th century.

The premise is that sound has, or even **is**, movement. Sound is heard movement; movement is visual sound. Music/speech has a grammar in movement. A consonant or a vowel for instance can be expressed by a movement, for example, for the sound of 'eee' the right arm rises straight above the head, while the left anchors straight down.

Hans Jenny summed up the phenomena of the effect that sound has on matter in *Cymatics: A Study of Wave Phenomena & Vibration*. He developed techniques to show that every frequency and musical note has a particular geometric pattern that it forms and David Tame in 'The Secret Power of Music' says that when looked at microscopically they are beautiful and mathermatically precise mandala structures.

This alphabet of sound – Eurythmy – was developed into performances in which a troupe of 'dancers' swirls and turn together to a piece of music or a spoken poem, rather like a corps de ballet 'showing'

131

the poem or music. The son of the house was a passionate student of Eurythmy and what I had seen on his desk were 'forms', as they are called, Eurythmy choreography, maybe of his own making. And yet I had recently seen such drawings coming from the dance temples of ancient Egypt and India! Steiner was clearly tapping into higher realities and into what is called the Akashic record where, it is said, all events from all time, past and to come are chronicled.

I knew a certain amount about Eurythmy having attended classes for the parents at the Steiner school, which my children went to, and had felt excitement both at its power and at that cellular knowing when something is true. It also felt extremely familiar!

A year or so before the connection was made for me between Eurythmy and the ancient sacred dances, I had been to a local alternative art exhibition; all I remember was the room of pyramids and the dancing!

I was with some of the chanting and drumming group Prana, and as they made music with drums and flute expressing the energy they felt in the room, my friend and I began to dance. We entered a trance state, danced by the energy of the beautiful pyramids and by the inspiring music. I was somehow aware that my body was moving in a way it had never moved before and with a grace and momentum and fluidity, with almost an urgency that was new, and yet to that tiny 'director' part of me who is always aware however high the experience, it was not new. I knew what I was doing! Not in this lifetime, but in ancient Egypt! The fabric of time had been pierced in that hall and I **was** a dancer in an Egyptian temple at the time of the pharaohs. I **knew** this stuff! I knew the significance of the swirls and turns I was making, the importance of the hand positions, of the angle of the head and the arms, the turning of the wrist. I knew this was not just dance to feel good; this was magical; this affected things consciously; this changed things.

What I have realised, through immersing myself in these experiences and in the Dance, is that in Sacred/Circle Dance a similar magical, alchemical process is happening. It is akin to the song lines sung by aboriginal people in Australia that hold things in existence, or the elaborate sacred sand painting in the Kalachakra[18] in the Buddhist tradition.

When the magical work of the Kalachakra ritual has been done the sand is scooped up and poured into the river; when the magical work of the dancing circle is done, the centre is packed away and the dancers go home.

I don't know if there will be a place for such detail in Sacred/Circle Dance in the future. I know I feel excited at the prospect of exploring this area of movement and magic.

Eurythmy performance.

On a Sacred Dance training course with Friedl Kloke[19] in Holland in the late 1980s she taught the **Sun Meditation** dance, which we all knew, but she made a subtle movement with her right foot at the end of making each sun ray and before beginning the next which was new to me. Yes! I shouted silently, this is what I came for! This is refinement! This is creating **precise** energy.

In the many recently choreographed dances where the dancers dance individually without holding hands, the dancers have the discipline of keeping the circle form energetically and knowing their place within it while being free to dance their own interpretation of the dance. Their arms and hands are free so they too can dance. Once arm and hand movements are available the possibility of magical precision comes closer.

The nearest I have come to this so far is in one of the dances that arrived using me as a conduit. It is called **Hex**. It was birthed quickly and fully formed, one of those experiences where, by-passing the thinking brain, you know exactly how something is meant to be.

I had this feeling that first time I walked the ancient labyrinth on the Swedish island and emerged from it, light years later, feeling I knew and understood everything, not in my head – that was empty – but in the cells of my body.

The power of **Hex** is in the opportunity it gives people to express what may never have had an outlet – their own deep, raw power. It is an extremely precise dance, a 'work' dance, and the more precise and disciplined the movements, the more powerful the energy raised. Thus the arm movements are strong, the hands straight to channel energy smoothly, and the eyes follow the movements so there is total awareness of what the body is doing at every stage, bringing consciousness into what is happening and teaching the power of intent and focus. An arm that is raised with limp fingers carries a very different message to the body from an arm raised with straight, but not rigid, fingers. One lacks direction and belief in the effect of what is happening, the other gives a definite, strong and positive message of '*Yes, I can! I am! I will!*'

24

Still Point
– moving to stillness and the quiet centre within

> 'Except for the point,
> the still point,
> there would be no dance,
> and there is only the dance.'
>
> 'The Four Quartets'
> T.S. Eliot

Crudely put, there are essentially two different approaches to 'home', centre, the still point – either by going down and in, or out and up: by focusing inside to find the spirit within, or by reaching up and invoking spirit to come down.

The way of the patriarchy has been the latter. Patriarchal religions like Christianity exemplify the dualist principle that matter, especially flesh, is evil, and spirit good, so matter must be suppressed in order to reach God/spirit. The old Christian way of the cross taught that redemption was only available through denial of the body, hence hair shirts, flagellation, celibacy, penances etc.

It was a way of pain and suffering, the way of their leader who was one in an established tradition of dying and reborn sun/vegetation gods who were whipped, humiliated, died painful deaths and then resurrected. The way to enlightenment was to deny the body and look upwards for help, aspire upwards to spirit, even though there was little or no chance that this state of nirvana would be reached while in a mortal sinful body anyway.

The icon of Jesus on the cross is usually placed up high for the faithful to reach up to, in eternal hope. At the time of the conquest and destruction of the First Nations of America by the whites, a ritual to bring spirit to the people was developed known as the Sun Dance. This still occurs annually in some tribes. Braves are pierced in the chest through the connective tissue at the pectoral muscles. This is done first with an awl and then with a sharpened cherry wood stick. Thongs are then attached through this opening and up to the central pole of the Lodge, or the tree cut specially for the ceremony. The braves then dance for four days without food or drink as their way to reach Great Spirit and intercede for their people.

Early in Christianity the Divine Feminine was split into the Virgin Mary and Magdalene the Whore; the first was portrayed as pure, unsullied, white and unattainable – quite beyond the reach of mere mortals, while the other was denigrated and permitted only as an eternal penitent forever confessing and suffering for her sins! The one an unattainable aspiration, the other eternally aspiring for forgiveness.

The true healed feminine knows the body to be a sacred temple that houses the spirit. It knows no separation between matter and spirit, it knows that all things are imbued with spirit, and that Truth is discovered by focusing inwards and finding the real Self within one's physical self, within one's own body.

The body of the dancing circle is a metaphor for the individual dancer's body. In both there is movement around stillness. The circle turns around a centre that does not move – (well, let's say, that **ideally** doesn't move! There is much joking in Circle Dance sessions about the way some dancing floors tilt causing the circle to slide off centre! And about those trickster centre altars which will keep moving around!) – so the movement of the dance parallels both the movement of the dancer through life and the constant movement within the dancer's body systems, the flow of the blood and lymph, the spiralling movement within each cell.

The centre of the circle is the place of non-movement, a still place, and this too is mirrored in the individual dancer; this is the small quiet place within which everything is known and understood, where opposites are brought into oneness, where personal truth and integrity reside, where the essence and the blueprint of the fully awakened Self connects with the physical body. Our still centre is always with us, always peaceful and pure no matter what turmoil surrounds it, even when we are so caught up with the movement around it we forget to be there in it, even forget that it **is** there.

The Dance brings together the polar opposites of movement and stillness, and teaches that movement can only be meaningful when it

136

The spiral power of the hurricane.

reflects inner stillness. And when there is this inner stillness the dances communicates their inner truth.

So when we dance, we find, as individuals, our own link to the Source and at the same time experience that our inner still point connects to the greater communal centre where as separate atoms we know unity with each other, with all people, and with all of life. It is from this centre point that we dance; it is the wellspring of our life here. It is through that point, like passing through the eye of a needle, that we come to know who we really are. All movement is contained in that small still seed. T.S. Eliot encapsulated it in these immortal lines:

> *'At the still centre of the turning world,*
> *Neither flesh nor fleshless,*
> *Neither from nor towards;*
> *At the still point, there the dance is . . .'*

137

25

Catalysing Change
– ways in which the Dance changes things for the better

> *'Wherever we stand on the circle we are at a turning point.'*
>
> Unknown

Returning to an earlier statement that circles 'keep things as they are' – energetically speaking the exact opposite is true in Sacred/Circle Dance. You could say that, far from maintaining what is, the aim of the Dance **is** to change things!

Curious that although tremendous change happens through Sacred/Circle Dance the number of Sacred/Circle Dance teachers and groups, according to the network quarterly magazine, Grapevine, does not! It reached a plateau several years ago and remained static. Strange, after such initial expansion.

But then our bodies, unless there is serious malfunction, do the same: they grow fast, reach optimum size and then stop! As do plants, trees, animals; every living thing comes with a blueprint for its growth, a built-in size regulator. It is a natural law and maintains an order and a balance, an order and balance which is currently being lost, violated by the cancerous giant companies which threaten to freeze the energy flow of the planet.

Outside the recorded network there continues to be expansion as the Dance is brought into so many areas by enthusiasts who introduce a dance here or there into what they are already involved with, be it education, prisons, health care, business conferences etc. It may be that the actual numbers of dancers has reached the size needed for optimum functioning, and is fulfilling its blueprint perfectly and effecting positive change. Who knows?

Movement and intent are the alchemical ingredients that create the changes.

We'll take a look now at ways in which the Dance is a catalyst for change.

Earth energy

In September 1984, as part of a Festival of Fountain International in Brighton, an experiment was made with a dancing circle and the energy lines of the area. In the vicinity of the dancing was a church, and the lines, which were discovered by the experienced dowsers[20] present, were strong.

All lines were dowsed and recorded and lines of force were found in the form of a cross, with a diagonal passing through the church. The 27 dancers came into a circle in the centre of the area and immediately the lines grew stronger. The first dance was taught – **Enas Mythos**, the simple Greek greeting dance, which traditionally started Dance sessions – and the lines grew to four in the form. During the dancing of this first dance the bands increased to seven. This dance was repeated and the bands then increased to eight.

This pattern continued through five more dances, some danced only once: the lines kept on increasing in strength, with a reduction to three and sometimes two between dances. The dowsers found that it dropped back with applause after the dance, so applause was vetoed, but clapping in rhythm, when it was part of a dance, had no such lowering effect on the energy lines.

The number of people in the circle was varied to see the effect and the dowsers found that the power of the energy increased as the size of the circle increased.

With 21 in the dancing circle and an inner circle of about ten in a group hug (people who felt in need of healing) the energy again went up. Then at the end, with approximately 50 standing in an outer circle just holding hands around them, there was a marked increase in energy levels. It was discovered at that point that there were eight bands of eight lines and, most importantly, that the main line had diverted from its former straight path to head for the nearby chapel, a move of 45 degrees.

This simple experiment confirmed, if confirmation were needed, that the Dance changes the energy around it. That the energy in the experiment was seen to revert to original strength as soon as the circle broke focus shows that the dancing builds energy, rather like filling a reservoir with water; that the energy grows as long as the dancing continues – provided the contact is maintained, and as soon as the reservoir/circle breaks the 'water' spills out.

Circles face inward, focusing on the space in the middle, just like chalices containing and building energy. The energy can be either 'positive' or 'negative' depending on intent. If the focaliser or leader has the conscious intent that the 'chalice' be filled with light energy and positive loving qualities, so it will be. If every person in that circle holds a similar intent the effect will be greatly increased. This is true even of a static circle, one that simply stands on the spot, but if a circle is dancing, moving in harmony and repeating movements over and over in rhythm, the power is hugely magnified. The difference in effect is as great as between a static water wheel and a wheel at a working mill. The water activates the wheel, turning it around and around so that it has the power to drive the machinery, which is, in turn, a series of turning wheels! Powerful effects from moving circles!

When a chalice is full it overflows: when the dancing comes to an end, the circle 'chalice' is full of light, with more continuing to flow down as the circle stands in a focused receptive state, until it overflows. This energy is either allowed to overflow from the circle as it will, or it may be directed.

The focaliser or teacher may speak the dedication at the end, sending the energy out, or it may be left, as is often the case, to happen in silence. In the early days I always ended Dance sessions with a phrase I was 'given' once when in a meditative space – *'We offer this dance to the Cosmic Dancer that the eternal harmonies be restored.'* Grand sounding stuff, and though it might sound weird to some, there was nothing, I felt, that could possibly give offence to anyone from any organised religion or belief system. Whether the energy is directed or is allowed to take its course, however, change happens, both for the dancers and for the area.

Transforming spaces

Sacred/Circle Dance teachers spend a lot of time changing unlikely, unpromising spaces into dance temples. Sessions are frequently in standard dusty village halls or church meeting rooms that boast one electric socket and strip lighting and are sprinkled with un-stacked stackable chairs! Transforming a dull room into a magical dancing space is one of my favourite activities! It's astonishing what can be achieved with scarves, bits of material, candles, and flowers; with colour, time, dedication and a little imagination!

One of the most challenging I have ever been faced with was a bare dead space in a warehouse in an inner city. To say it was unlovely would be a compliment. Old dusty brick walls, linoleum on the floor, windows, yes, it did have windows, but almost opaque with grime, and of course the ubiquitous strip lights! To create a dance temple required a team of enthusiasts, a couple of hours of hard work and a carload of equipment!

In came cases of shawls, scarves, sheets, sarongs, boxes of candles, night lights and zillions of holders; vases and armfuls of flowers, both table and standing lamps, incense, sticky tape, drawing pins and a couple of electric fans, as it was discovered that the windows didn't open more than a crack. All had to be hauled along corridors, up two flights of stairs, along more corridors, through several doors that threatened to take an arm off as they snapped shut with only half of you through! But it was worth it! The transformation happened, the place was changed and not only on the physical level: the energy of the place was changed!

Energy hoovering

Looking at the energy pattern formed by a dancing circle, it is shaped like a vertical cylinder. Energy is being raised up from below and at the same time it is being grounded from above. Putting that on hold for a moment – there is a cosmic energy pattern called a torus, known also as a 'doughnut' as that is its shape. DC electricity passing through a loop creates a magnetic field – (circle dancing power!) If the lead is wound into a coil, the magnetic field creates an imploding and exploding doughnut, or 'torus'; the power moves continuously over the top and down into the middle, out at the bottom, around, and up again.

The pattern of the magnetic energy around the earth is a 'torus'. We are all living in a doughnut! A dancing circle with its vertical cylinder of coiled electric power creates a 'torus' of magnetic power, which draws energy in from round about it. What this circle becomes is an alchemical pot, Cerridwen's cauldron[21], in which unloving/disruptive energy can be drawn in and transformed.

Back to the water wheel – every tread on the wheel is like one of the dancers in the circle doing their bit to bring energy into the centre of the wheel which then moves the drive shaft, which then activates the vertical vortex, which then activates the torus.

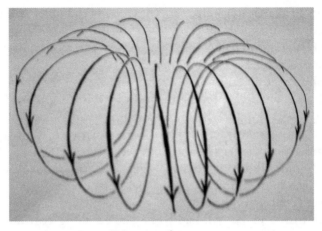

Diagram of a torus.

Moving from water wheels to moths, to bring in another strand – moths, creatures of the night, are drawn to light – *'like moths to a flame'*. The compulsion is so strong that if they make for a flame, they usually immolate themselves in it. In a similar fashion unloving/disruptive energy may be drawn to the light that is generated in a Dance circle; pulled into the centre on the 'torus' swirl, transformed, and passed out again as positive energy. It's like a giant washing machine, but rotating vertically.

So what is this energy and where does it come from? Baldly put, it is the absence of truth. It is dark and unloving energy destructive to the spirit, that is generated from thoughts and actions of hatred, greed, jealousy etc., which in turn are all cancers produced by fear. Perhaps 'negative' energy can be described as the uncontrolled results of fear. If these 'negative' forces pile in, unchecked, on top of each other around a person or a place, they can grow into thought forms which can eventually become strong enough to be able to operate on their own. They feed from unloving, untruthful human thoughts and feelings, so they fly around seeking someone to feed off and operate through. If ignored, they can over time become demons – the stuff of nightmares. The way they operate is in stealth in the dark, through the subconscious: once seen and recognised, they lose their power and their form disintegrates. All that is needed is for them to be brought into the light of consciousness.

A dancing circle is generating the vibration of love and shining a bright light, which can attract 'moths of darkness' and transform them into neutral or positive energy. Two things to make absolutely clear: one is that, to my knowledge, no dance circle sets out with the intent of attracting and disabling this sort of energy – it happens! The other is (and I have no way of verifying this, it is a feeling), only a fraction of circles are even conscious of this, and it may well be – again I surmise only – that this sort of 'hoovering' only happens when there is awareness of the phenomenon, by, at least, the focaliser.

People changing

The change that is blatantly obvious to all Circle dancers is the positive changes for individuals that come from this form of dance. The most immediately obvious is the release of tension. Suddenly you're not holding everything together all on your own, suddenly the realisation penetrates that you're not alone, that you are a piece of something bigger, an integral part of a moving, coherent, joyful, supportive whole. Tight muscles relax, suspicious stressed lines soften into smiles. Often when someone dances this way for the first time, they have a feeling of 'At **last**!' a sense of relief at having found their tribe, their spiritual home.

As there is no hierarchy in a circle, there is freedom to be yourself, to follow your heart and your own knowing, to accept **yourself** as the authority on your life. You simply learn a few steps and the circle dances you! This allows you more and more to trust **life** to dance you! The experience may, for some, be the first time they have known acceptance in their lives, the first time they have felt validated not only as a unique individual but also as a necessary and valued part of something bigger than themselves. Gradually confidence grows in themselves, in the ability to run their life, to make choices freely and above all to open to life and to others and allow love in.

When I began to Dance I really started to know myself, to feel strongly the guidance in my life and sense my place in the great scheme of things. I took hold of the Dance, like Ariadne's thread, and change happened! First inwardly, then like a river in spate that couldn't be held in, it burst out, exploding a marriage that had belonged to the person I had thought I was. I followed the thread through the ensuing aggression and the seemingly impossible thickets of a bitter divorce. It knew the way, every step of it, and always has, even when nothing has made any sense and there has been no suggestion of a track in any direction. I have never let it go and it still continues to guide me into knowing who I truly am and into the freedom to really **be** who I am and dance my own dance within the holding of the Great Circle.

In the Dance we meet many aspects of ourselves.

We may be surprised at the effect on us of, for instance, a warrior dance, having never before felt that particular energy of focused power or channelled aggression; it may have been repressed very early in order to model the perfect well-behaved child for our parents.

We may be uncomfortable, embarrassed even, at the heat and body sensations that come from moving the hips in a sensual 'Gipsy' or 'Rom' dance – products, that we are, of effective Victorian and Christian repression of sex!

We may soften our defences and weep while dancing a heart-focused, heart-opening dance. We may cringe or feel angry at dancing one of the old dances about the acceptance of female subservience to men. We may meet and have to reconcile the battling energy that seeks change, with the quiet acceptance of things the way they are.

Each dance has its own special quality, its own unique vibration and this may connect with and awaken that particular vibration in the dancer. Taken collectively in a Dance session they are a formidable barrage of catalysts for change. The effect is to create wholeness within the psyche, a re-connection of forgotten, repressed areas, and to forge an impermeable link with the Greater Self.

Political change

Many Sacred/Circle dances come from Eastern Europe – old Yugoslavia, Russia, Romania, Armenia, and Hungary. Some dancers when they experience dances from another country have a strong empathy with them, feeling that they are familiar, that their bodies know how they are to be danced. Many have direct awareness of having lived in the country in a previous life.

I recall a time somewhere around the end of the 1980s/beginning of the 1990s when there was an interest in the clothes that the dancers wore in the different countries and areas. Somehow traditional costumes from Macedonia were acquired and tried on and a few of the women wore them to dance in. The consensus was they were too restricting to be comfortable for modern women but wearing them certainly gave a sense of the style of the dances, dictating, for example, how big or small a step should be.

There was, and still is, a strong sense of the people whose dances we enjoy, a 'feeling into' their lives, and empathy with the repression and hardship the women endured. There is no doubt in my mind that this deep connection with the spirit of these countries and the regular dancing of their folk dances in the spirit of kinship, contributed to the melting of the Iron Curtain when the folk spirit of these countries erupted giving the people back their freedom and the dignity to live their own culture. In the time that Sacred/Circle Dance has been flourishing – from the early 1980s on, enormous political changes have happened in Europe.

We have seen the coming down of the Berlin Wall, the break up of the Soviet Union and the reclaiming of sovereignty of small swamped countries and ethnic groups. I feel certain that dancing the dances of such countries and such groups, with focus, in the loving ambience of a circle, empathising with the pain of the people, and holding the truth and beauty of their culture, helped to keep their spirit alive and to facilitate their freedom from dominance.

In a passage in '*The Book of Laughter and Forgetting*', Milan Kundera is watching circles dancing in the streets of Prague in 1950, two years after the Communists seized power in his country. As he watches one circle of laughing singing people their steps speed up, and as in a vision he sees the circle rise up from the earth; higher and higher they go still dancing – '*a wonderful wreath of bodies rising above the city*'; over the executions and the '*jails full of traitors*' and '*they had wings*', '*they were flying like birds*'. When I first read this I saw it as the culture and folk spirit of the Czech people rising above the Communist state and the indomitable soul of the people lifting through the repression.

This was how I chose to interpret it and it still inspires me, and whether or not it is Kundera's intent, it is still how I see the power of the Dance and the work of positive energy. First, the Dance creates a vortex to clear 'negative' energy; secondly instead of taking the way of confrontation to effect change (which, as energy follows thought, actually increases the problem through the focus brought to it), it facilitates positive change by simply focusing the attention on creating an alternative reality, on restoring the 'Circle', and on building it with truth, with love and with positive intentions.

If we look at the make-up of the brain we can see how we create whatever we think and focus on. Our brains have intricate networks of interconnected thoughts. There is a positive network linking positive thoughts and experiences together and a 'negative' network linking 'negative' experiences. If something happens that makes us feel depressed, for instance, this will link in with all the 'negative' experiences and thoughts we have ever had. Unchecked this becomes an avalanche that depresses us even more. When we dance we reverse this. Why is it we always feel so much happier, calmer and energised at the end of a

Dance session than when we came in? – the dancing gives us joy, peace and love and so our brain links up with the whole gamut of all our enjoyable peaceful and loving experiences, thoughts and memories.

Interconnectedness

To illustrate further that moving circles catalyse change, it is only necessary to look at what is now known about the relationship of the individual to the whole. We are learning the hard way that we are not isolated entities but part of a web that connects all life forms on the earth, that all things are interrelated, that all cells of the body are interconnected, that the earth is a single organism, a body, made up of an infinite number of cells.

A hive of honeybees, a colony of ants, each of these is a single unit. Each bee, each ant is a cell of a whole. The whole is contained in the cell, the cell contains the whole – the universe, as William Blake puts it, in a grain of sand. Microcosm and macrocosm – whatever we do affects every body and everything else: a tremor or an explosion somewhere on the earth reverberates, sending waves through the entire web. According to the chaos theory and Edward Lorenz butterfly effect[22] a butterfly flapping its wings energetically and activating the molecules of air around it in Japan could be responsible for 30-foot high waves off the California coast because everything is connected on a deep level!

We are learning the truth of this interrelatedness in the 'negative' '*I sneeze, you catch a cold*' sense; it is as true in the 'positive' sense.

What is happening is that this oneness of life, which we have known intellectually and embraced as a concept for so long is now being experienced in daily life. We are **living** those well-aired maxims like '*there is no such thing as separation*'; '*we are each other*'; '*if I hurt you I hurt myself, if I bless you I am blessed*'. Life is making sure in our everyday experiences that we are finally getting it on all levels!

Following a serious car crash on a motorway there was the usual back up of miles of traffic and the usual amount of frustration and cursing at the delay. A woman, alone in her stationary car a few hundred metres from the crash, however, thought of the people involved in the accident and sent up a prayer for them.

Another woman lay seriously wounded in one of the mangled cars. The wounded woman slipped out of her body and floated up seeing the scene below – the wrecked cars in one of which her body lay, the three lanes of still vehicles stretching into the distance. None of it felt important to her anymore, she was travelling up into the light, but then she noticed that one car was glowing with light and she knew that inside it someone was praying for her. There was a sharp tug on the cord that still connected her to her physical body and slowly she began to return. She memorised the number plate of her rescuer's car and later when she had recovered, wrote to thank her. We are one another!

This is a one to one situation, one individual affecting another; widening the lens. Maharishi, who brought Transcendental Meditation to the West, maintains that it only needs 10% of a community, town or country to meditate in order to change the whole unit and create a peaceful and love based community, town, country. It's the story of the magnet and the iron filings all lining up in the same direction; the story of the hundredth monkey – when the hundreth monkey learns a new skill all the others in the 'tribe' automatically acquire it.

Energy follows intent so it follows that how we choose to see things is vital. And it **is** a choice – we can see violence and hardship as the reality on earth or we can choose to see *'the love that underlies the happenings of the time'*. Whatever we choose we will create. Is the theatre half full or half empty? We can see an industrial wasteland or we can see the beauty and strength of the earth beneath the surface ugliness. Attitude is what counts. Seeing and holding the truth and the Reality behind and beyond appearances is the key to creating change. Focusing, as the dancing circles do, on what is eternal, on being in the present, on love, on beauty, on what is true, on the unity of life, is what creates real, positive, lasting change.

Imagine 10% of the population of the earth dancing Sacred/Circle Dance – Meditation in Movement – and see how the earth glows and the vibration of the planet shifts to love and truth. This is my vision for the future and yet the reality is that it is all here now. Sacred/Circle Dance takes us into what is eternal, but if it's eternal, that means it is also here now. In the eternal Now! This is the Garden of Eden, heaven is here on earth right now, the rest that we see are simply shadows and they are rapidly dispelling in the Light of the One Dance.

26

The Dance Goes On!

– summary, and looking forward

'*We dance not for ourselves but for the good of all people*'

Zumi people of N. America

People have always danced; danced to ensure the earth would feed them, danced in thanksgiving, danced to celebrate, to express grief and joy, danced to build courage, to strengthen community, danced to merge with their god or goddess, danced their dreams.

At this time in the human story we are seeking union, a bringing together of the fragments of ourselves, and of ourselves as atoms of the one being: a return to wholeness. Barriers, borders and divisions between people, beliefs and polarities are being challenged; what is sacred, what is secular, and are these divisions appropriate now, what indeed is **not** sacred? What makes a movement or a space or indeed anything sacred is our intent, is the meaning we bring to it, and it is this consciousness that makes Sacred/Circle Dance a unique and valuable tool for healing, growth and transformation.

The Dance operates on both a personal and a universal level; it works on the physical, mental, emotional and spiritual level of the individual dancer and strengthens the immediate community and its effect is worldwide. In the circle, the dancers are facing in to the sacred centre, to Source, to spirit; they circle a tenemos or sacred temple space – a safe and loving and familiar world created by 'solo' or 'spirit-family'; their backs are to the outside world, the world out there; they are the eye of a storm, an oasis of tranquillity and truth in a chaotic world. They stand and dance between two worlds, building the energy of the inner world to lift the vibration of the outer world, as the healing effect of the energy ripples out across the whole earth.

Vibrations exist at an immensely faster level than our bodies. What happens through the Dance, as through other spiritual disciplines, is that the vibration level of the body is being raised until it eventually reaches the level of the spirit. This is why the body often feels lighter when dancing this way, and why at the end of an evening there can be a sensation of floating and of not being made of earthy substance at all. At these times, the soul or spirit, the higher part of the self comes into the physical body and the dancers experience that what in fact they are made of is purely energy.

The physical body is the vehicle for the soul, yes, but at such times the **actual cellular structure** of the body is changed and becomes light – light not only in the sense of not heavy, but Light. Through the dancing the strands of the dancer's own personal web are strengthened and harmonised so the cells of the body can transmute it to its true state, to its resurrected state; this is happening now while we are still alive on the earth, while we are still in the physical body. This is what Jesus meant when he said, *'if thine eye be single, thy whole body is filled with Light'*, in other words the dancers experience their true dimensions, and become the angels they are!

Mother Meera, an Indian embodiment of the energy of the Divine Feminine, lives in Germany, in the heart of the corporate industrial world, and gives 'darshan'[23] to hundreds of people four nights of every week. This darshan takes place in total silence and the pilgrims who come to her from all over the world each leave with a strand of the Divine Mother energy which they carry, usually unknowingly, back with them on their journeys home, so creating new energy patterns and strengthening the web of light over the planet. The Dance likewise is creating and strengthening the web of light and the lines or fibres of light from each circle radiate out across the earth as healing power; each circle builds this energy, and each teacher, bringing her or his own unique way and insight to the Dance, creates a special strand in this web of light that is being woven worldwide.

Sacred/Circle Dance brings inner and outer into harmony together; it balances the world of doing with the world of being, gently leading the dancer into deeper consciousness of the energy behind form; it creates and promotes the qualities of the feminine to balance the over emphasis on the masculine in our world; it aligns us with the vertical as well as the horizontal planes of life; it brings us to the still point of timeless reality and spiritual truth; it catalyses change for individuals, for the collective and for the earth; and it brings us back into awareness of the many circles of our lives and the Great Circle of the One Life.

I have felt, and do feel, immensely grateful to all my own teachers along the Way for what they gave me and for their unique gift to this web of dancing light: in the order in which they touched me – to Bernhard for The Gift; to Taras for handing me the thread; to Colin Harrison for quiet authority, focus and dedication; to David Roberts for precision and for opening up the world of Dance as Ceremony; to Anna Barton for simple and clear teaching style; to Maria-Gabriele Wosien for embodying the sacred; to Friedl Kloke for wisdom, grace, poise and centredness. I feel deeply privileged to be part of this great unfolding adventure. I feel, too, compassion for all those who teach and who have come through the tests and trials of their dancing journeys over these years of serving the Dance. They have kept faith! As Bob Dylan sings – '*I'm going all the way, till the wheels drop off!*' And how far it has all come! And how awesomely gentle has been the guidance each step of the way. '*And the Dance goes on and is never ending, the circle turns and returns again . . .*'

Dancing at sunset on Dorset beach.

27

Dance Steps

Code

Line 1 – direction of dance (arrow)
direction nose facing (nose)

Line 2 – long beat _ , short beat ᵁ
Line 3 – foot. R, L – right foot, left foot.
Line 4 – what the foot does.

F	forward
B	back
S	side
Cl	close
Li	lift
XF	cross in front
||	|| repeat

Enas Mythos (see page 69)

Face centre holding hands with left arm crossed over right. Step forward on left foot, close right foot to left and let the knees bend slightly twice (two quick little bobs). Step backwards on right foot, and as the left closes to it, again two little knee bends; step sideways to the right on right foot, and as the left closes finish the sequence with the two little knee bends.

Island of Kos, Greece — Forearms crossed L over R

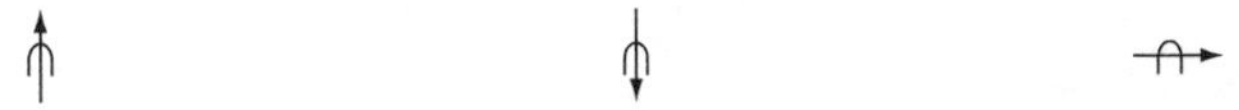

L R 2 knee bounces	R L 2 bounces	R L 2 bounces
F Cl	B Cl	S Cl

Omal Garassari (see page 71)

Greece   V hold

R L ‖ R L L R ‖ ×2
F F   S Cl S Cl

       heels stay together
       turning body side to side

Tsamikos (see page 40)

Greece   W or shoulder hold

    ─∩─►   ◄─∩─

    _ U   _ U _ U _ U
‖ R L ‖ ×3 R L ‖ L R   L   R
  S XF   S Li S XF S Li

Name from Klephts clothing (bands of men in the Greek mountains waging guerilla warfare against Turks and Albanians in the Greek War of Independence). Whole outfit is call Tsamika. Now often danced by men and women together sometimes even led by a woman. The tone is lonely courage and the hardships and brotherhood of the Klepht life.

White Bird (see page 103)

Dance – June Watts.   Music – Bolivia   V hold

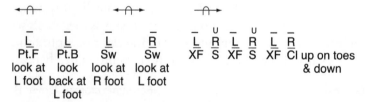

  _   _   _   _   _ U _ U _ _
  L   L   L   R   L R L R L R
Pt.F   Pt.B   Sw   Sw XF S XF S XF Cl up on toes
look at look look at look at   & down
L foot back at R foot L foot
       L foot

June's dances

The steps for June's choreographies mentioned in chapter 18, Birthing Dances, are available from the author – june@junewatts.com.
Web site 'www.junewatts.com'

Endnotes

[1] Philip Thornton 1910–92. One of the greatest pioneers and researchers into Balkan traditional dance, was the first Westerner to record the dances of Romania, Bulgaria and Yugoslavia, in the 1930s. Founder member-teacher of the SIFD in London, in the 1940s. The first to invite a group of Romanian villagers to England (to the Albert Hall in 1937). Author of three classics: 'Voice of Atlas', 'Ikons and Oxon' and 'Dead Puppets Dance' (Collins). Enormous influence on Sacred/Circle Dance through his teaching of traditional dance to early members.

[2] Terpsichore comes from two Greek words 'terpsis' – joy, and 'horos' – dance, song, theatre.

[3] The Grapevine currently contains 24 pages, and is mailed to 750 subscribers.

There is a four-step sequence in Sacred/Circle Dance called a 'grapevine'; this comes from the Middle East where it is a dance symbol for water; it is a winding and flowing step reminiscent of the winding of a vine. Vines grow and spread at a phenomenal rate too like the Dance! And they bear fruit!

A team of people – volunteers – produces the Grapevine and the team changes every couple of years or so. Grapevine currently costs £3 an issue and contains listings, groups, events, musicians who play for the Dance, and teachers both in Britain and worldwide. Teachers can advertise their events there. It also includes Dance and music information, news, ideas, history, stories, poems etc.

Other countries – USA, Germany, South Africa and Holland – produce their own periodical magazines.

[4] This is from Bernhard – Findhorn Sacred Dance paper 1976.

[5] Tsamikos – originally from Epirus, now THE Greek man's dance par excellence; in 3/4 rhythm, leader does acrobatic variations to show his virility and that of the villiage. Usually in 12 or 16 steps.

[6] Taize is an international, ecumenical community founded in 1940, in Taizé, France.

[7] Laban created a theoretical system called eukinetics, which was intended to increase the dancer's control of dynamic and expressional movement so he/she could perform a wide variety of dance styles with expression and control.

[8] I am reluctant to talk of energy in terms of negative or positive meaning: one is good and the other bad. Energy that is called negative in the sense of bad is an energy without love, it 'negates' love, truth and life. 'Live' denied or reversed becomes 'evil'. As there is a negative and a positive charge in electricity it does not feel appropriate to use these same terms to denote what is considered bad or good. In the context of electricity one is not good and one bad, they are two halves of a whole, polarities, which together make power. To differentiate between the two I have used inverted commas in the text to indicate negative or positive in a judgmental sense.

[9] See the research and experience of Dr. Batmanghelidj in his book 'Your Body's Many Cries For Water' (www.watercure.com).

[10] Nightlights, the little candles in an aluminium holder, are called 'tea lights' in Canada! Puzzling! Canada is not known for its Russian emigrants so it's unlikely that they are called tea lights because they keep the tea warm in the samovar. Further research is needed on this!

[11] Omal Garassari is a Pontic dance. Pontus was an ancient country on the shores of the Black Sea, North-east of Asia Minor (now Turkey). In 1923, there was an exchange of populations with massacres and military actions on both sides, Orthodox Christians in Turkey and Muslims in Greece were exchanged according to the Treaty of Lausanne. Pontic Greeks are now to be found all over Greece, especially in the north and in Athens, trying to keep their culture.

[12] See Dance Steps section page 152.

[13] Music from Gula Gula by Marie Boine Persen, Realworld CDRW 13. Dance notes from author.

[14] Dora Stratou. Grand lady of Greek traditional dance. With some help from others, she, almost unilaterally, saved it from decline, by carefully recording dances, collecting costumes, listening to stories, often from the last villager who kept the tradition.

[15] 10000–5000 BC.

[16] The fire walking ritual is an ancient pagan event which has become Christianised. Banned in 1960 by the Communist government it was allowed back in the 1980s as a tourist attraction.

[17] The flowers were Galium verum, lady's bedstraw.

[18] This exquisite and elaborate Kalachakra mandala needs great skill from the Tibetan monks. Using metal funnels for the coloured fine sand it takes them months to create. The mandala is dedicated to peace and physical balance, both for the individual and for the world and is for a ceremony to focus healing for the earth. The mandala is three-dimensional, a five-storeyed 'divine mansion', at the centre of which stands the Kalachakra deity, the manifest state of Enlightenment. Simply seeing this mandala creates peace on many levels. According to the Dalai Lama, the Kalachakra deities reduce tension and violence in the world. *'One doesn't need to be present at the Kalachakra ceremony in order to receive its benefits,'* he explains.

[19] Friedel Kloke-Eibl A principal disciple of Bernhard Wosien, followed in his footsteps teaching traditional dance and creating superb choreographies. At one time founded and directed the only school in this branch of Sacred Dance. Has published videos of her choreographed rituals, and many CDs on Sacred and traditional dance. An authority on ballet, Greek dance etc. Visited Findhorn with Wosien, pioneered sacred dance sequences for the community. Teaches in many countries, based in Germany.

[20] Dowsers use either a pendulum suspended from the hand, which swings in different directions to indicate a 'yes' or a 'no' to posed questions, or two metal rods held loosely one in each hand in front of the body. The rods will turn up or down, or in or out, in response to the intent.

[21] Cerridwen is the Celtic triple goddess of maiden, mother and crone and the cauldron is the vessel of regeneration.

[22] In mathematics and physics, chaos theory deals with the behavior of certain nonlinear dynamical systems that (under certain conditions) exhibit the phenomenon known as chaos. An early pioneer of the theory was Edward Lorenz. He first analyzed the effect in a 1963 paper for the New York Academy of Sciences. According to the paper, 'One meteorologist remarked that if the theory were correct, one flap of a seagull's wings could change the course of weather forever.' Later speeches and papers by Lorenz used the more poetic butterfly, possibly inspired by the diagram generated by the Lorenz attractor, which looks like a butterfly. Wikipedia Encyclopedia.

[23] Darshan, in the Hindu tradition, is a viewing of a Guru or Enlightened Master or Avatar which is believed to convey blessings. Each person at the darshan with Mother Meera kneels at her feet while she lays her hands on the head; as she removes her hands the devotee looks up into her face until she lowers her eyes signalling it's time to make room for another.

Further reading

Sacred Dance	Maria Gabriele Wosien
Subtle Body	David Tansley
The Secret Power of Music	Daniel Tame
Sacred Woman, Sacred Dance	Iris Stewart
Mystic Spiral	Jill Purce
Science and Human Transformation, Intentionality and Consciousness	William A. Tiller
Vibrational Medecine, the no. 1 Handbook of Subtle Energy Therapies	Richard Gerber
The Power of Now	Eckart Tolle
The Permaculuture Way	Graham Bell
The Secret Power of Music	Daniel Tame
Cymatics: A Study of Wave Phenomenon and Vibration	Hans Jenny
Divine Harmony: the Life and Teachings of Pythagoras	John Stroheimer and Peter Westbrook
A Beginner's Guide to Constructing the Universe	Michael S. Schneider
The Findhorn Garden – pioneering a vision of humanity and mature in co-operation	The Findhorn Community
The Power of Myth	Joseph Campbell
Pathways to bliss and personal transformation	Joseph Campbell

Further reading

Awakening to Zero Point	Greg Braden
An Actor Prepares	Stanislavski
Avebury Cycle	Michael Dames
Eurythmy: Rhythm, Dance and Soul	Thomas Poplawski
Mandalas and their Meaning in your Life	Suzanne Fincher
The Healing Labyrinth	Helen Raphael Sands
Walking a Sacred Path	Lauren Artress

About the author

Movement is the keynote of my life. When I was a child the family was constantly on the go! My father's work moved us on every three or four years; he was a minister in the Methodist Church whose policy was to keep its employees on the move. Whether this was so they wouldn't put down roots or so the faithful wouldn't have to put up with a third rate priest for too long, I do not know; what I do know is that I learnt that life was about moving on; about packing up, saying good bye, meeting new experiences – endlessly moving on. It suited my energy patterning though, having been born under 'mutable air' with both my sun and moon in the sign of Gemini. I just wasn't built for a static predictable life.

I enjoy the process of creating a life situation for myself, living within it for a while, then letting it go and moving on. This 'butterfly' mentality invoked severe criticism from my parents who saw my exploration of one new thing after another as superficial flitting. *'Why don't you settle down and get yourself a steady job!'* The artist Brueghel saw hell one way and portrayed it in graphic detail; my picture was and still remains a little different! It's composed of a 9–5 job, security, and an existence in a box in a row of identical suburban boxes, knowing what my life will look like in 10, 20 years from now!

Theatre was my passion from childhood on and remained so until full time parenting took me over. The theatre life suited me just fine; always on the move, changing towns and theatres, roles and work mates, always exploring new aspects of life and of myself through the many and various parts I played. The butterfly's wings were clipped with motherhood though; no more going where the wind blew, and the flowers she alighted on were the same three little flowers in the same little patch of garden.

In the first year of marriage (to an actor who brought back home with him the smells and chatter and excitement of the theatre which kept a feeling of connection for me), I trained as a Natural Beauty Therapist, an absorbing experience which not only explored the make up of the body and skin and how to make natural creams and remedies but also opened the door to many alternative realities. We touched on natural diet, astrology, acupuncture and energy flow, Ayurvedic body types, palmistry, reincarnation, the Kabbalah and much more; it was an Aladdin's cave of delights for me, it opened my eyes to a different world view and I have delighted in following up each of these delights during my life.

It also meant I had a life of my own – as a masseuse; in Warwickshire when the Royal Shakespeare Company was in its Stratford-upon-Avon home, and in Fleet Street (an exhausting succession of beery, stressed journalists with bodies as relentless as brick) when it was in London. While loving the role of parent and frequently feeling fulfilled by it there were times of intense longing for theatre as the ultimate creative expression of my soul.

The birth of my first child, a daughter, catalysed a monumental inner crisis, through which I was led to a healing service in a Spiritualist Church and received a profound experience of my soul crying for recognition and telling me of my purpose here as a woman dedicated to spirit. I was on the move spiritually.

Just after the birth of my second child, a son, I was initiated into Transcendental Meditation which was a life saver and kept me from breaking up under the pressure of two then three small children as a single parent most of the time as their father was wedded to the theatre. This opened the way for me to explore my own way of spirituality which eventually took me away from the local C. of E. church I had been attending in the village outside Stratford, through a time at the Spiritual Community Church of Rudolph Steiner until I was ready to let go and dive into my own limitless spirit.

Some of the most exciting times in my theatre life were the musicals and pantomimes primarily because of the dancing. I Charleston-ed in '*The Boy Friend*', did top-hat-and-cane 'high kicks' in '*Oh, What a Lovely War*', comic and sweet-young-thing routines in pantomime rep. (provincial repertory theatre), waltzed elegantly on Broadway in the Royal Shakespeare Company's '*All's Well that Ends Well*', and danced full-bloodied rock in Trevor Nunn's seminal '*Winter's Tale*' at Stratford, in Japan and Australia. High times, when I felt fully alive.

Movement during the motherhood years was racing around keeping up with three small children; up and down stairs, to the shops and back, to school and back and on and on; and no applause! Then, miraculously, when the smallest child was two, I found myself on a weekend of many kinds of dance; someone had rubbed the jar and my creative genie had popped out. It was all an amazing treat but during a two hour slot of something called 'Sacred Dance', I burst into life more fully than ever before; this was what I had been waiting for all my life, without knowing it.

Three years ago in search of a simpler life close to the earth, my partner and I moved to a mountain in Spain! Now I have two 'incarnations' going on side by side – one as an international Dance teacher, the other a Spanish peasant. They are dramatically different, in fact diametrically different but it suits a dual 'Gemini' subject, and one day – the famous 'mañana' day – the vision is that the two will come together, and dancers will come here to form a sacred dancing circle and soak up the peace and healing of these beautiful mountains.

June Watts